DEMOCRACY IN PREWAR JAPAN

Groundwork or Façade?

DEMOCRACY IN PREWAR JAPAN

Groundwork or Façade?

EDITED WITH AN INTRODUCTION BY

George O. Totten

UNIVERSITY OF SOUTHERN CALIFORNIA

D. C. HEATH AND COMPANY
Lexington, Massachusetts

Library of Congress Number: 65-19459

Table of Contents

Introduction

DEMOCRACY is the central tenet of our political faith in America today. We desire to be more democratic than we are and we want the rest of the world to be democratic too. But what are the conditions that make for a predominantly democratic society? Studying the case of one society where whatever democracy there was failed or was crushed could provide insights into conditions prerequisite for democracy and into what we really mean by "democracy."

The Japan that attacked Pearl Harbor in 1941 was motivated by an ideology incompatible with democracy, an ideology that positively opposed it along with individualism, egalitarianism, liberalism, socialism, communism, anarchism, and other "Western" concepts. Even the term "fascism" was looked down upon, though "totalitarianism" was held in high repute. The nation rallied behind the imperial mission and supported an emasculated one-party system. The vast majority of the people dutifully voted during the war for the candidates for the Imperial Diet "recommended" by Premier General Tōjō. The Japanese government and people were united in believing that they possessed a unique *kokutai* (national polity or essence). Actually, how the ideology of the immediate prewar and wartime periods should be described poses a difficult question, which is discussed in another volume of this series: *Japan 1931–1945: Militarism, Fascism, Japanism?* edited by Ivan Morris.

Was it, in any event, inevitable that Japan should attempt a totalitarian regime and eventually line up with Nazi Germany and Fascist Italy? In the First World War

Japan had joined the Allies (albeit by a close decision) in the war "to make the world safe for democracy." Earlier, the Japanese government had promulgated a constitution and borrowed much from the democratic West in terms of legal codes, political parties, and newspapers as vehicles of public opinion, certainly not only from a desire to be accepted in the comity of "civilized" nations but also because many really desired these things for the sake of a better life. Clearly, new groups were struggling toward greater participation in the political process. Why did they not succeed? *Could* they have succeeded, given the general conditions in Japan and the world at large? This is the central question of this book of readings.

Many have expressed themselves on this question. Their qualifications for evaluation range from the uninformed businessman tourist to the learned Japanese scholar who has studied the experience and wisdom of the West seeking the answer. Yet even the opinions of the latter cannot be accepted as final; he may be reading into history something that is relevant to his own experiences, and consequently the phenomena he examines might impart a different meaning to any of us, since we may be seeking answers to questions phrased in terms of our own historical background and present needs. This holds especially true when we are dealing with a subject such as democracy which is so difficult to define. It might seem at first that we should decide on our own definition of that concept and then set forth with that, employing it as a standard by which to discard all studies which do not use the same criteria. But would not such an approach bar us from insights we might eventually wish to incorporate into our own understanding of the idea?

Each author included here has his own concept of democracy. Most of them are implicit and it would constitute an exercise in deduction to discover them. Professor Scalapino, however, quite explicitly states that his definition establishes two criteria: "(1) adherence to the concept of the innate dignity of man and recognition of his total development as the ultimate goal of the state; and (2) acceptance of choice as the fundamental qualification of democratic institutions, with positive protection for civil liberties, a competitive party system, and the other necessities of an 'open society.' "

The first of these criteria may be called a "content" definition and the second a "process" or "mechanism" definition of democracy. The first specifies positive principles. Variations may emphasize types of equality, such as political, economic, and/or racial. Others stress only a theoretical equal opportunity, perhaps to compete in a "free enterprise" system or to be judged before the bar of justice without prejudice. Under this heading come also those definitions which glorify the "general will." Variations of the second criterion may emphasize majority decisions, popular participation, the parliamentary system, or limitations on them of one kind or another. Perhaps these two types of criteria cannot be separated in practice, but they can be useful analytically in evaluating whether and to what degree democracy existed in prewar Japan, or for that matter, in any society at any particular time.

While it is hoped that this collection may provide the reader with insights into the meaning of democracy in general, its specific aim is to present informed, if conflicting, descriptions and evaluations of democracy or its potentials in two seminal periods in recent Japanese history. The first period was that of the "liberal" movement which developed in the 1870's and 1880's. Known in Japanese as the *jiyū*

minken undō or "freedom and people's rights movement," it is often referred to as the "democratic" or "populist" movement or even by other names. The other democratic thrust centered on the 1920's and is referred to by an even greater array of designations, such as "Taishō democracy," "the normal path of constitutional government," "the realization of universal suffrage," or "party rule."

The first of these movements resulted in the granting of the Meiji Constitution in 1889, the creation of the Diet (as the Japanese parliament is usually called in English) in 1890, and the development and consolidation of political parties during the next decade or so. But evaluations of these institutions and their operation revealed that they fell far short of standards of democratic practice as found in such Western nations as England, France, or the United States at the time. The Meiji Constitution's "guarantees" of civil liberties contained fatal loopholes, the Diet's powers were severely circumscribed in both theory and practice, and the political parties proved to be willing to call off the struggle for a share in the decision-making process in return for comparatively insignificant rewards from the real power holders.

The second democratic thrust began perhaps with the stirrings of discontent after the passing of the Meiji emperor in 1912 and reached its first crescendo at the end of World War I. Wartime business had boomed, but many people had suffered and eventually vented their blind fury in the rice riots of 1918. The government fell and the first non-titled, genuine party leader became prime minister, inaugurating what many hoped was a period in which the democratic potentials of the Meiji Constitution would be realized. Many hoped for the acceptance of the principles that the prime minister should be chosen from the majority party and that he should enjoy pre-eminence in the decision-making process. But to establish such principles, the powers of various other constitutional and extra-constitutional bodies would have to be curtailed. At the same time the moral prestige of the lower house would have to be enhanced to enable it to claim to represent a mandate from the people, which could only be done if the members were elected by universal suffrage.

In retrospect, it was to be seen that all these drives achieved only partial success and by 1932 the current turned against such democratic, parliamentary advances. The outbreak of the China Incident in 1937 released a torrent that in 1940 swept away all the independent political parties and rendered the parliamentary process mere ritual. Why had all this occurred? Was it inevitable?

Various clues to the complex answers to these questions will be found in the pages of this book. An overview of the whole modern period prior to World War II is provided by a selection from a study by Dr. Edwin O. Reischauer. He places great weight on the creation of parliamentary institutions and rates highly their operation in the 1920's as the arena wherein the increasingly pluralistic interests of Japanese society adusted or fought out their differences. In his view, only a slight shift in the balance of forces, due to the confluence of a number of external and internal trends, knocked the center of gravity again away from the path of constitutional development.

Thereafter the focus of the readings comes to rest on the first period under consideration, with a summary and evaluation of it by the two most important leaders of the early liberal movement, Counts Itagaki and Ōkuma. They attribute much greater importance to their own efforts in pressuring the Meiji oligarchs to grant a constitution and parliament than does Reischauer, however much they concede concerning the shortcomings of the parties as they had developed up to the time of the Russo-Japanese War of 1904–5. The movements they led are then analyzed by two of the foremost scholars on this period, the late Dr. Norman and Dr. Ike. The former emphasizes the limitations of the movement

due to its agrarian character as differentiated from the urban liberalism of England which had brought about laissez faire and limited government. Dr. Ike paints a clearer picture of the ideology of this movement, arguing that it not only frightened the ruling oligarchs but also the leaders of the movement itself, including Itagaki and Ōkuma.

The section on "Taishō democracy" and the decline of "party rule" opens with views on the prospects of democracy in Japan by two of its most prominent advocates at the time. Professor Yoshino, scholar and polemicist, worked out a theory of democracy that would harmonize with the main tenets of the "emperor system" in Japan, building on the work of Minobe Tatsukichi, the foremost liberal scholar on the Meiji Constitution. His study and first-hand observations of democratic practices abroad gave him great faith in the possibilities of adapting the essentials of democracy in Japan for the benefit of the country. In contrast, Ozaki Yukio, politician par excellence, while sharing many of Yoshino's views, was more impressed with the specific obstacles to parliamentary government. He tried to emphasize the positive aspects of practices as they had developed so far in Japan, such as the collective responsibility of the cabinet in certain regards, but he was almost in despair over the factional nature of Japanese political parties against which he struggled all his life.

Two observers then comment on subsequent democratic developments and aspirations. Lecturing in 1924, Mr. Tsurumi, who subsequently became a Diet party leader, gives the inside view of a liberal on the evils of big money in Japanese elections and the fervent hopes for amelioration that universal suffrage would bring. Seven years and three general elections after the enactment of manhood suffrage, Professor Quigley gives us his penetrating observations on the characteristics of the parties and the dilemmas they faced. The disillusionment over the lack of change brought about by the extension of the suffrage has already set in, but the parties are still seen as the only hope for democratic development.

Finally, two postwar scholars, one American and one Japanese, reexamine the potentials in this second period. Dr. Scalapino, noting the close relationship between the development of capitalism and the rise of middle-class democracy in the West, traces the growth and behavior of the business classes in Japan. He finds them at first all too dependent on the state up until the First World War. Thereafter they do operate increasingly through political parties; but with the coming of the world depression and the initiatives of the military abroad, they acquiesce in a war policy and the emasculation of the parliamentary system. By way of contrast, Dr. Ishida places less weight on the weaknesses of capitalism in Japan and focuses attention on the power structure. He attempts to account for the movement of political parties toward increasing democracy, such as their struggle for universal suffrage and party rule, while recognizing that they also functioned to channel control downward from the government, dominated by bureaucrats, to the people. He reasons that, when the bureaucrats found alternate lines of control through officially sponsored mass organizations, the parties lost even this second function and thus became superfluous in the eyes of the gradually changing power elite.

In the final section — Evaluation of Japanese Democratic Potentials — three contrasting hypotheses are presented. Here Professor Scalapino draws out the implications of his earlier analysis, emphasizing the unfortunate timing of Japanese industrialization, and attempts to refute alternate causal explanations. Dr. Yanaga, an American scholar of Japanese ancestry who can thereby penetrate the inevitable barrier that surrounds the "foreigner" in Japan, staunchly refuses to concede that the Japanese have gone through the kind of fundamental revolution in *Weltanschauung* that enabled the Western countries to transform themselves from feudal to modern democratic societies. Fully disagreeing, Dr. Reischauer not only believes that the Japanese left the essence of feudalism behind by the time of the Meiji Restoration of 1868 — which he prefers to call a revolution — but that feudalism itself contained positive elements that helped propel Japan into the modern world. Thus, he does not view democracy, even in prewar Japan, as having been in conflict with the remnants of feudalism so much as with new totalitarian trends that have emerged as a result of the process of modernization itself. He leaves us with the thought that this fundamental struggle, endemic in all advanced societies, is still going on. By implication, therefore, the present collection of readings on democracy in prewar Japan has wide relevance today.

A NOTE ON TECHNICALITIES

In Japan the family name comes first and the personal name last. There are no middle names. Since the Japanese name order was used by almost all the authors included here, it has been adopted in the table of contents as well. However, the names of Americans of Japanese ancestry are given in the usual English order.

Another problem with Japanese names is that of variations in reading the Chinese characters that stand for their names, especially their personal names. An example is Hara who became premier in 1918. If one were not familiar with the arbitrary reading of the character for his personal name, he would pronounce it in the "Chinese" fashion, Kei. Hara's father actually decided on Satoshi as the reading for this name.

But that was not widely known, and as a result many people used a more common reading for this character, Takashi, in romanizing his patronimic. This explains variations here regarding Hara's and others' personal names. Alternate readings are indicated in the Glossary.

The long mark over certain vowels in romanized Japanese (not used by all the authors) indicates that the sound is prolonged. It does not signify an accent or a change in the pronunciation of the vowel. Each vowel is pronounced uniformly. The value of Japanese vowels is similar to the Italian, for example.

At this point, I should like to acknowledge Professor Ivan Morris' help in planning this book.

GLOSSARY

ABE ISOO (ISOH) (1865–1949). Moderate socialist theorist and politician. A graduate of Dōshisha University, he became a Christian and remained one throughout his life. He studied in the United States, where he finally became a moderate socialist. He was one of the founders of the abortive Social Democratic Party in 1901. Later he helped establish the Social Democratic Party of 1926 which lasted until 1932 when it merged with other proletarian parties to form the Socialist Masses Party. Abe became chairman of that party until 1940, when he retired from public life.

AIKOKUSHA (Society of Patriots). Formed in 1875 by Itagaki to oppose the government but was forced to disband shortly afterwards because Itagaki was lured back into the government.

BAKUFU. Literally "tent government," it refers to the regime of the Tokugawa Shogunate, 1603 to 1867.

BLACK DRAGON SOCIETY (Kokuryūkai). More correctly the Amur [River] Association, this was an aggressive ultra-nationalist group founded in 1901. It was dissolved at the end of World War II.

BOKU RETSU AFFAIR (Summer, 1926). A Korean nationalist, Boku Retsu (known by this Japanese reading of his name, which was really Pak Yŏl in Korean), was arrested for a minor matter, but during his interrogation he boasted of having planned with his Japanese wife to harm the Emperor. For this he was sentenced to death and his wife, to life imprisonment. Premier Wakatsuki commuted his sentence to life imprisonment, considering that the difference in sentences between husband and wife might be construed by Koreans as discrimination against Koreans. But Wakatsuki was attacked by the opposition on the grounds that he was being soft toward Korean nationalists and thus endangering Japanese control over Korea.

BUSHI. Another word for samurai or warrior or knight.

BUSHIDŌ. The Way of the Warrior (or Samurai). This term did not gain much currency until the twentieth century, though it is supposed to describe the code of ethics of the samurai during feudal times.

CHŌSHŪ. See SAT-CHŌ.

DIET. The word usually employed to translate *gikai* which means parliament in Japanese.

DŌSHIKAI. See RIKKEN DŌSHIKAI.

ELDER STATESMEN. See GENRŌ.

"EMPEROR SYSTEM" (TENNŌ SEI). This refers to the bureaucratic structure of the Japanese government capped with the Emperor. The whole system rests on reverence for the Emperor; accordingly, even the lowest bureaucrat considers himself a representative of the Emperor and that his authority ultimately derives, however tenuously, from the Emperor. Although the Emperor possesses all power, he never acts except on advice. Therefore, "direct access" to the Emperor gives the person who has this prerogative (such as a Genrō) the highest authority in a wide sphere.

ETŌ SHIMPEI (1834–1874). An anti-Shogunate member of the Saga Clan, he helped organize the new Meiji government and aided in the introduction of laws based on the French civil code. In 1873 he resigned from the government and joined Itagaki and Soejima in a memorial to the throne asking for a people's assembly, but then, in 1874, he joined in the insurrection against the government, was captured, and beheaded.

FUKUZAWA YUKICHI (1834–1901). A business leader with Western and liberal convictions, he espoused English utilitarianism and championed moderation. Influential in politics, public opinion, and education, he established a great newspaper and founded Keiō University in Tōkyō. As a superb publicist and indefatigable translator, he had an immense influence on Japanese intellectual and political life.

GENRŌ (Elder Statesmen). This was the group of oligarchs that carried the mantle of responsibility of governing Japan during the Meiji period and after. It included Itō Hirobumi and Yamagata Aritomo. Itō's protégé, Saionji, was adopted into the group and became its last "member." This group preceded the Meiji Constitution and its power was "extra-constitutional." Gradually its members died off toward the end of the Meiji period and during the Taishō period, except for Saionji, who died in 1940.

GOTŌ SHŌJIRŌ (1837–1897). A leader of the Liberal Party (Jiyūtō) 1881–4. Previously he had joined Itagaki in calling for a people's assembly.

HAMAGUCHI OSACHI (Yūkō) (1870–1931). Politician. After graduating from Tōkyō Imperial University he entered the bureaucracy but changed his career when elected to the Imperial Diet in 1915 as a member of the Kenseikai. He was Finance Minister in Katō Takaaki's cabinet. Became leader of the Minseitō in 1927 when it was set up. Became Premier in 1929 and softened Japan's foreign policy which had been aggressive under the previous Tanaka cabinet. For this he was shot by an ultranationalist and later died from this wound the following year.

HARA SATOSHI (The Chinese character for his personal name is often read Kei or Takashi.) (1856–1921). In 1918 he became the first commoner and first professional politician to become Premier.

INUKAI TSUYOSHI (Ki) (1855–1932). A somewhat liberal political party leader. After graduating from Keiō, he became a journalist. He joined the Kaishintō in 1882. During the Ōkuma-Itagaki Cabinet of 1898, he became Minister of Education. Thereafter he was often found in the ranks of the vocal opposition leaders, with Ozaki Yukio, who called for protection of constitutional government. He became Communications Minister in the Katō coalition cabinet that passed manhood suffrage. Yet in foreign policy, he was close to the line of Tōyama Mitsuru (1855–1943), leader of the Black Dragon Society. Like Tōyama, he had helped Sun Yat-sen but came to support Japanese aggression in China. While he was Premier, the state of Manchoukuo was set up. As head of the Seiyūkai, he was the last politician to become Premier in prewar Japan on December 13, 1931, but on May 15, 1932, while still in office, he was assassinated by ultra-nationalists.

ITAGAKI TAISUKE (1837–1919). Born into a Tosa clan samurai family, Itagaki joined the anti-Tokugawa forces and entered the Meiji government. He resigned along with Saigō Takamori over the government's refusal to launch an expedition against Korea in 1873, but he kept his opposition within legal limits and pressed for representative government (the so-called people's assembly) in 1874, declining to join Saigō's insurrection in 1877. He organized several patriotic societies, which were ultra-nationalistic in foreign affairs but concerned largely with welfare for the samurai who had lost their privileges as a result of the anti-feudal measures of the Meiji government. Gradually his movement took on a more liberal tenor, adopting slogans from the French revolution. In 1880 he formed the Liberal Party (Jiyūtō), the first national political association in Japan. The Jiyūtō was formed in an environment that had known only court intrigue or covert conspiracy. His own followers were mixed; some were samurai so steeped in feudal traditions that they had little idea of liberalism, others, so desirous of a new way of life they had no trust in the Meiji regime. Itagaki proved to be an untrustworthy leader, easily abandoning his followers for government favors. In 1889 after he and Ōkuma had finally combined to oppose the government, the oligarchs gave the two surprised leaders the task of forming a cabinet. It was shortlived, however, as they fell out with one another, but in a sense this was the first party (Kenseitō or Constitutional Party) government in Japan. Most of the members of that party were absorbed into Itō Hirobumi's Seiyūkai in 1900, and Itagaki's political career came to an end.

ITŌ HIROBUMI (1841–1909). The father of the Meiji Constitution. Influenced especially by Bismarck. Leader of the "civilian" faction as opposed to the "militarist" faction of Yamagata within the ruling oligarchy. He was assassinated by a Korean.

JIYŪTŌ. See Liberal Party. More accurately but less commonly, Liberty Party.

KATŌ HIROYUKI (1836–1916). A liberal who by the 1870's had become a conservative nationalist. In his early period he favored English liberalism; in his later period, Prussian absolutism.

KATŌ TAKAAKI (KŌMEI) (1860–1926). Statesman. After marrying into the wealthy Iwasaki family, he quickly rose in the Mitsubishi combine. Later he alternated service as Ambassador to England with being Foreign Minister. During his fourth time in the latter capacity, he prepared the Twenty-One Demands made on China in 1914. Disliked by the oligarchy, he finally succeeded in organizing the coalition cabinet of 1924 for the protection of the constitution, the first cabinet really created through the power of the parties. While he pushed through manhood suffrage and attempted reform of the House of Peers, he also saw through the "anti-subversive" Peace Preservation Law. Following the breakup of the coalition, he formed a cabinet based on his own Kenseikai Party. He died in office shortly thereafter.

KAISHINTŌ (REFORM OR PROGRESSIVE PARTY). Organized by Ōkuma in March 1882 and more or less dissolved in 1885. Descendants of the party eventually became the Minseitō of prewar Japan and even the Shimpotō (Progressive Party) of postwar Japan.

KATAYAMA SEN (1859–1933). A pioneer socialist in Japan who became a Communist and a high member of the Comintern. When he died in Moscow, his bier was carried by Stalin. As a youth of twenty-five, he journeyed to the United States to study and there became a Christian interested in settlement work. He helped found the labor movement in Japan and was one of the organizers of the abortive Social Democratic Party of 1901. Often traveling abroad, he left Japan for the last time in 1914.

KATSURA TARŌ (1847–1913). A protégé of Yamagata's of the Chōshū clan; a military man, bureaucrat, and statesman, he alternated with Saionji as Premier from 1901 to 1913.

KENSEIKAI (Constitutional Politics Association, 1916 to 1927). A political party, led by Katō Takaaki until he died in 1926 and then led by Wakatsuki Reijirō until 1927.

KIYOURA KEIGO (1850–1942). A bureaucrat-politician. A supporter of Yamagata Aritomo, he became a Count in 1922. In January, 1924, he became Premier but in June had to step down in the face of the attack by the three-party coalition led by Katō Takaaki. This ended his political career.

KENSEITŌ (CONSTITUTIONAL PARTY). Formed in 1898 by Itagaki and Ōkuma, but disintegrated quickly when the joint cabinet fell that same year.

KOKUMIN DŌSHIKAI (National or People's Comrades Association, 1929 to 1932). A minor political party which emerged from the Jitsugyō Dōshikai (Business Comrades Association) which had been formed in 1923.

KOKUMINTŌ. See RIKKEN KOKUMINTŌ.

LABOR FARMER PARTY (RŌDŌ NŌMINTŌ, abbreviated as RŌNŌTŌ). The first of the proletarian parties tolerated by the government after the passage of universal manhood suffrage in 1925. It was formed in March 1926, but as it became more radical, groups split off from it to form the Social Democratic and Japan Labor Farmer Parties toward the end of 1926. The Labor Farmer Party weathered the first Diet election under manhood suffrage in 1928 but was then ordered disbanded by the government. It was reconstituted in a much weakened state in 1929 and then known as the "new" Labor Farmer Party until it merged with another proletarian party in 1931.

LIBERAL PARTY (JIYŪTŌ). Formed November, 1880, by Itagaki and reorganized in October, 1881, it was dissolved in 1884. A reconstructed Liberal Party was formed in 1889 without Itagaki. But in 1890 Itagaki organized the Rikken Jiyūtō (Constitutional Liberal Party), known simply as the Liberal Party. Dissolved in 1898, its descendant was the Seiyūkai, formed in 1900. The Liberal Party in postwar Japan can trace its lineage back to Itagaki.

MEIJI. Literally, "Enlightened Rule," reign name of Emperor Mutsuhito (1852–1912) from 1868 to 1912.

MEISEIKAI (Bright Politics Association — April 17, 1928, to January 21, 1930). A small political party, led by Tsurumi Yūsuke, who, in the first election under manhood suffrage on February 20, 1928, had been elected to the Diet as a very "liberal" independent. There were peculiar circumstances in the Diet when the party was formed, and it played a peculiar role. Premier Tanaka had dissolved the House because his party, the Seiyūkai, did not have a majority and he hoped he could get one by holding new elections. However, he garnered only 219 seats to the 217 of his main opponent, the Minseitō party. The other thirty seats were distributed among independents and minor parties. Tanaka then used every means, including corruption, to win over enough of these other votes to avoid a nonconfidence vote by his opponents. In this he succeeded, and among those coming over to his side were Tsurumi and the other six members of his newly formed Meiseikai. This was a great shock to many liberals who had expected him to oppose the "reactionary" Tanaka cabinet to the bitter end. They therefore dubbed his party a "monster" or "chimera" (*nue*).

MINOBE TATSUKICHI (1873–1948). Prominent professor of law at Tōkyō Imperial University and one of Japan's most distinguished legal scholars. Around 1935 he was violently attacked because of his "organic theory of the state" (formulated twenty-five years earlier) in which the Emperor institution was considered an organ of government. As a result he was forced to retire from the House of Peers and from public life.

MINSEITŌ. One of the two main political parties during the 'twenties and 'thirties, the other being the Seiyūkai. Literally, "People's Political Party."

NARA JAPAN. This refers to Japan during the Nara period from 710 to 784 when Japanese culture was characterized by overwhelming borrowings from China.

NATIONAL POLITY (KOKUTAI). Sometimes translated as "national essence" or "national entity," it has a mystical meaning and refers to the unique relationship of the Japanese people to their emperors who have ruled over them from "time immemorial."

NISHI AMANE (1829–1897). He was sent to Holland by the Tokugawa Shogunate to study Western learning. Subsequently he spent his life introducing Western ideas into the milieu of Japanese culture. For instance, he helped Yamagata Aritomo draft the Imperial Rescript to the Soldiers and Sailors.

ŌKUMA SHIGENOBU (1838–1922). Born into the Hizen clan which joined the anti-

Shogunate forces. Ōkuma was one of the founders of the Meiji government. Ōkuma with his command of Dutch and English, his speech-making abilities, and impressive personality, might have become the leading figure in the Meiji Era. Fortunately for the development of democratic trends, however, Ōkuma was forced out of the government by the more powerful Satsuma and Chōshū clan bureaucrats who were jealous of him. The occasion of his being forced out was his memorial to the Emperor in 1881 calling for the establishment of representative government. He then organized the Progressive Party, as an opposition force, against the government but did not want to unite with Itagaki and his more radical following. Actually Ōkuma spoke for a wide segment of opinion, one which grew over the years, after the opening of the Diet in 1890 when he struggled to voice "public opinion." His prestige grew until he became Premier in the First World War. Ōkuma founded Waseda University in 1882 as a private institution financed by business interests. It became known for producing the best journalists and leaders of public opinion. His philosophy was close to that of his friend Fukuzawa Yukichi.

ORGANIC THEORY OF THE STATE. Rather than the biological organic view of Herbert Spencer who drew on Darwinism, the metaphysical organic theory came to Japan and was remolded and used by Minobe Tatsukichi and others more conservative than he. This metaphysical organic theory can be traced in the West back to Aristotle and St. Thomas Aquinas. Like the biological theory, it emphasizes interdependence, but its main point lies in claiming that the state is a moral organism.

OYABUN-KOBUN. Japanese for "father-like"–"child-like" or "father-role"–"child-role" reciprocal obligations, which can exist in many relationships such as those between leige lord and vassal, boss and henchman, patron and protégé.

RIKKEN DŌSHIKAI (Constitutional Comrades Association, 1913 to 1916). A political party formed from elements of the Teikokutō and Rikken Kokumintō; led by Katsura Tarō until his death in 1913 and then led by Katō Takaaki.

RIKKEN KOKUMINTŌ. (Constitutional Nationalist or People's Party, 1910 to 1922). Formed from elements from the Kensei Hontō, a split-off from the Kenseitō, it was reorganized in 1913 and lasted until 1922 under the leadership of Inukai Tsuyoshi; then it became the Kakushin Kurabu (Reform Club).

RISSHISHA (SOCIETY FOR FIXING ONE'S AIM IN LIFE). Founded by Itagaki in 1874 and soon dissolved.

SAIONJI KIMMOCHI, PRINCE (1849–1940). A member of the Genrō or Elder Statesmen, in fact the last one. A descendant of the court nobles or kuge, he studied in France as a youth and was then influenced by liberal ideas. As Itō Hirobumi's protégé, he became Premier twice, and was then gradually accepted as a Genrō. He loathed the rise of militarism in the 1930's and advised moderation.

SAMURAI. The Japanese version of the European warrior or knight.

SAKURADAMON AFFAIR (January 8, 1932). Four weeks after Inukai had set up his cabinet, a Korean nationalist Ri Hō-shō (Japanese reading of his name which was Yi Pong-ch'ang in Korean) threw a hand grenade at the Emperor who was passing near the Sakurada Gate in Tōkyō on his return from reviewing troops. Only slight damage was done but the Premier at first thought he should submit his resignation until the Cabinet Secretary-General Mori Kaku persuaded Saionji to suggest to the Emperor that Inukai be asked to stay on as Premier in view of the gravity of the problems that faced the government, such as the Manchurian Incident and the ban on the import and export of gold. Only the Tōkyō Metropolitan Chief of Police resigned, taking the responsibility for the affair.

SAT-CHŌ. Short for Satsuma and Chōshū clans, the two most important of the

Tozama or Outer Lord clans that overthrew the dominant Tokugawa clan and effected the Meiji Restoration. The two lesser clans that cooperated in this effort were the Tosa and Hizen.

SATSUMA. See SAT-CHŌ.

SEIYŪKAI (or Rikken Seiyūkai). A political party (literally, "Society for Political Friends of Constitutional Government") formed from the ruins of the Liberal Party (Jiyūtō) in 1900 by Itō Hirobumi. With certain transformations, it lasted until 1940. Even after World War II its "descendants" can be traced.

SHAKAITŌ (RICKSHAMEN'S PARTY). Organized in Tōkyō in 1882. If the "sha" in Shakaitō were written with a homonym meaning "social" instead of "ricksha," the result would be "socialist party." This connotation was probably desired.

SHIMPOTŌ (PROGRESSIVE PARTY). Formed in March, 1896, by Ōkuma. A descendant of the Kaishintō (also Progressive Party), it was an ancestor of the Minseitō.

SHINTŌ. "The Way of the Gods or Kami." The earliest pantheistic religion of the Japanese, it did not receive this name until the coming of Buddhism in the sixth century, A.D., at which time it was greatly influenced by that more sophisticated and philosophical religion.

SHIZOKU CLASS. The samurai class.

SHŌWA. Literally, "Enlightened Peace," the reign name of Emperor Hirohito (b. 1901) from 1926.

SOCIAL DEMOCRATIC PARTY. See ABE ISOO.

SOCIAL MASS PARTY. See SOCIALIST MASSES PARTY.

SOCIALIST MASSES PARTY (SHAKAI TAISHŪTŌ). Formed in 1932 by a merger of the other legal "proletarian" parties. It excluded Communists and "national socialists." In 1940 it was the first political party to dissolve itself voluntarily to make way for the one-party rule of the Imperial Rule Assistance Association, which, however, never did get any real power.

SOYEJIMA (ALSO SOYESHIMA OR SOEJIMA OR SOESHIMA) TANEOMI. A liberal of the 1870's and 1880's.

TAIKA (OR TAIKWA) REFORM. The Japanese attempt in 645 A.D. to remodel the government along the lines of the T'ang empire of China.

TAISHŌ. Literally, "Great Righteousness," reign name of Emperor Yoshihito (1879–1926) from 1912 to 1926.

TAKAHASHI KOREKIYO (1854–1936). Statesman. His education was capped by an unhappy trip to the United States before the Meiji Restoration. Upon his return, he served as a minister of state in various capacities and then went into banking for a while. After returning to politics, he became Prime Minister and President of the Seiyūkai upon the death of Hara. He gave up a peerage to fight in the constitutional protection movement and then served in the coalition cabinet of Katō Takaaki. With the onset of the depression, he represented zaibatsu financial interests in his oft-held post as Finance Minister, calling for retrenchment of the military budget. He was one of those assassinated during the February 26 (1936) Incident.

TANAKA GIICHI, GENERAL, BARON (1853–1929). Premier 1927–9. A "militarist" associated with the so-called "Tanaka Memorial" (see below). Under his Premiership a fierce suppression of "communists" took place and a deterioration of civil liberties.

TANAKA MEMORIAL. This was a memorial supposedly submitted by Premier Tanaka Giichi to the Emperor on July 25, 1927. It is now considered a forged document and yet it was based on much valid material apparently from secret deliberations.

TEIKOKUTŌ (Imperialist Party). Also known as Kokumin Kyōkai (National Association) and Daidō Club, a Diet party of the 1890's.

TENNŌ. This means "Emperor of Japan." Literally, the "Sovereign of Heaven." It was not the term used in China for Emperor, nor is it a generic term which would mean emperor for any other country.

TOKUGAWA ERA. The period of 1603–1867, so named because hegemony was in the hands of the Tokugawa clan, while the Emperor was in fact powerless.

TRANSCENDENTALISM. This refers to the practice of creating supra-party, non-party, or "transcendental" (*chōzen*) cabinets, that is, cabinets that "stand aloof" from the parties. This constitutes, of course, a negation of the principle of party cabinets (in which the Premier is a party leader), not to mention "party rule" (in which the Premier is the real political leader of a single-party or coalition majority in the Diet).

UEKI EMORI (1857–1892). A journalist and democratic theoretician for the Liberal Party (Jiyūtō).

YAMAGATA ARITOMO (1838–1922). Known as the "father of the army" because he introduced conscription and modern training. He was a rival of Itō Hirobumi's. Twice Premier. A Genrō.

YAMAKAWA HITOSHI (KIN) (1877–1958). Socialist theorist. Attended Dōshisha University; became a journalist; but soon became a socialist. For his beliefs, he was arrested and sentenced several times. He was a leader of the "first" Japanese Communist Party, but by 1927 he opposed the party as a leader of the "Labor Farmer Faction" (Rōnōha). In 1922 he had urged socialists widely to work for mass support and utilize the parliamentary process for revolutionary ends. He remained a leading socialist theorist until his death.

YAMAMOTO GOMBEI (1852–1933). Career navy man and politician. Became a Count and Admiral. Originally from Satsuma. Formed his first cabinet (1913–1914) after the third Katsura cabinet, his second (1923–1924) almost a decade later.

YOSHINO SAKUZŌ (1873–1933). Graduated from Tōkyō Imperial University in 1906, he was appointed assistant professor there three years later. He traveled and studied in Europe and America from 1910 to 1913. Though he resigned his professorship in 1924, he was considered one of the foremost political scientists in the Japan of his day.

The Conflict of Opinion

OVERVIEW

"[F]or more than a decade after the First World War the Cabinets were largely party Cabinets. . . . The carefully controlled revolution of the Meiji period was developing into a runaway liberal movement of the urban middle classes."

— EDWIN O. REISCHAUER

THE PEOPLE'S RIGHTS MOVEMENT, THE DIET, AND THE EARLY PARTIES

"It was the political parties who first created the public demand for the establishment of a national assembly and . . . forced the Government to act constitutionally."

— ITAGAKI TAISUKE AND ŌKUMA SHIGENOBU

"[T]he agrarian movement . . . was the core of early Meiji political life in the broadest sense . . . ; when directed against usury, high rents and excessive taxation, it expressed a vague aspiration toward a fuller democracy. . . ."

— E. HERBERT NORMAN

"From the point of view of the government this was a formidable movement because it had a more than rudimentary party organization and because one of the most important elements in it were the wealthier landowners and rural industrialists who had a firm grip on local government. . . ."

— NOBUTAKA IKE

"TAISHŌ DEMOCRACY" AND THE DECLINE OF "PARTY RULE"

"It is improper to reject democracy on the grounds that it limits the emperor's sovereignty and is therefore bad."

— YOSHINO SAKUZŌ

"[T]he customs and usages of feudal times are so deeply impressed upon the minds of men here that even the idea of political parties, as soon as it enters the brains of our countrymen, germinates and grows according to feudal notions. . . ."

— OZAKI YUKIO

"The politics of Japan would have been far more liberal had it not been for the enormous expenses involved in parliamentary elections. . . ."

— TSURUMI YŪSUKE

"It is the favorite cry of liberals in Japan to-day that the parties are effete, corrupt, quarrelsome, selfish — in general disreputable . . . Granted the truth of these criticisms, what was to be expected from the materials with which the parties have had to build and in the presence of the obstacles, constitutional and administrative, with which they have had to contend? . . . However, no agencies other than the parties exist to fight the people's battles."

— HAROLD S. QUIGLEY

"In its failures as well as in its strengths, Japanese capitalism was of too little service to the democratic cause."

— ROBERT A. SCALAPINO

"[P]olitical parties, including the proletarian, constituted no more than a subsidiary means of control between the supra- and infra-structure of the 'emperor system.' . . . Nevertheless, for a time 'the normal path of constitutional government' was more or less operative, and certainly a possibility . . ."

— ISHIDA TAKESHI

EVALUATION OF JAPANESE DEMOCRATIC POTENTIALS

"In short, the industrial revolution was condusive to more than one political expression, depending upon the timing and intensity of its development."

— ROBERT A. SCALAPINO

"Westernization in the political sphere at best was little more than a superficial imitation of European and American institutions. . . . This resulted in a multiplicity of façades which served to obscure if not conceal, especially for the casual or superficial observer, the traditional concepts and attitudes that were much too deeply rooted in the nation's past to be readily superseded by alien ideas and ways of doing things."

— CHITOSHI YANAGA

"Japan in the past hundred years has witnessed not just superficial modifications but a fundamental social as well as economic and political transformation. . . . Culturally a bourgeois revolution had already taken place in [Tokugawa] Japan, and the economy, despite the feudal façade, was in many ways an early capitalistic economy. . . . The two forces of democracy and totalitarianism are inevitable concomitants of machine production and universal education. . . . The struggle between [them] . . . goes on."

— EDWIN O. REISCHAUER

OVERVIEW

The Rise and Fall of Democratic
Institutions in Prewar Japan

EDWIN O. REISCHAUER

To present a sketch of the rise and fall of democratic institutions in pre-World War II Japan, one of the foremost Japanologists has been chosen. He is one who not only dares to write forcefully but who believes that a democratic groundwork was actually constructed in prewar days.

As Professor of Japanese at Harvard University, Dr. Reischauer taught and wrote about the whole panorama of Japanese history from the earliest times. But because of his outstanding ability and his special concern for an American foreign policy that would build on Japan's democratic heritage and strengthen her ties in political, economic, and cultural matters with the United States, he was appointed United States Ambassador to Japan in 1961, the first who knew the Japanese language, the first expert on Japanese history, and the first who had a Japanese wife. He himself had been born in Japan and lived through part of the period he writes about here.

Perhaps Dr. Reischauer can be classified among those scholars who believe that the essence of democracy lies in familiarizing people with the parliamentary process in such a way that they learn to vote intelligently for those political parties responsible for making governmental policy decisions. Whether or not this is a completely fair classification, he seems to be saying in this selection that before World War II, the Japanese people did have the requisite institutions for the development of democracy, and that increasing numbers of them were participating in government especially since the 1920's, but that the militarists and ultra-nationalists took advantage of certain constitutional flaws to thwart the functioning of the system. He goes on to point out, however, that the business groups, the bureaucracy, and even labor were not wholly or strongly committed to democracy.

More specifically, Dr. Reischauer points to the more complex character of the ruling groups that replaced the earlier tight-knit oligarchy by the end of the First World War. Struggling among themselves, these high-level bureaucrats, both civil and military, sought support through political coalitions with politicians backed by urban zaibatsu and rural gentry. In this way, the Diet became a key instrument of government, but it soon lost this role because of a number of institutional flaws, chief among which was the theoretical supremacy of the emperor which could be more easily used by ultra-nationalists than liberals for their own ends. Other subsidiary flaws included the limitations

From Edwin O. Reischauer, *Japan: Past and Present* (New York: Alfred A. Knopf, Inc., 1946), pp. 147–151 and (Third Edition, Revised, 1964), pp. 123–125, 142–153, 156, 158–159, and 162–178. Reprinted by permission. [All the selection titles in this book are the responsibility of the editor. This and other readings in the book appear without the footnotes which are found in the original publications.]

on the Diet's power over the budget and the military bureaucracy's direct access to the Emperor. In addition, Dr. Reischauer does not neglect to mention other internal and international factors that brought about the demise of democratic developments in pre-World War II Japan, but the significance of his interpretation lies in his strong affirmation of the existence of a democratic groundwork.

Whether Dr. Reischauer's interpretation is valid or not is for the reader to decide with the help of this and other books and articles. But let us not forget that there is no such thing as a completely "factual" history, because even the mere selection of the "facts" involves interpretation as to their relevance, if nothing else. Ideas as to what is relevant or important are continually changing.

Consequently, history is constantly being rewritten. This is not only true in societies which have controlled presses but also in those that are free. Historians themselves often change their own evaluations in the light of new materials and new explanations by others and also in the light of their own further experience, hindsight, and perspective. Lucky is the historian who has a chance to rewrite an earlier study of his own.

In bringing out a revised edition of his 1946 survey history of Japan, Dr. Reischauer has done just this. In the following excerpts, a few of the places where he made relevant revisions have been indicated; the original passages have been reproduced in italics. These reveal that his evaluation of prewar democracy has somewhat mellowed. His analysis of the Japanese attempt at totalitarianism has also become more complex, but in this case his new passages are expansions on more laconic statements in the earlier version. As they do not affect his evaluation of democracy in prewar Japan, they have not been indicated.

T HE new [Meiji] government was in essence an oligarchy in the hands of fewer than one hundred young men. They had no reason to be dissatisfied with their own form of rule, but they saw the advantages of many Western political concepts and institutions as essential adjuncts of government in any strong state. These features of the West they borrowed in rapid succession. They created ministries on Western models in one administrative field after another; and they organized a prefectural system of rule which kept the control of each prefecture in the hands of the Tokyo government. They adopted the Western calendar, but held to the old Chinese system of counting years by "year periods," which beginning with the Meiji "year period" became identical in duration with the reigns of the emperors. They adopted a policy of religious toleration, permitting the propagation of Christianity once more; they modernized the police, the currency, and organized a modern postal system; they revised and standardized the tax system, and created a national banking system, first on American and then on European lines; they established a civil service; and they revised the legal system and courts on French patterns. Finally, they established a Cabinet on the German model, and even drew up a Constitution for Japan, providing for a parliament called the Diet.

The last step showed that the oligarchy was at last broadening the basis of its rule. But unlike the constitutions and parliaments of Western lands, which had usually been the result of popular demand and pressure, the Japanese Constitution and Diet were the gift of the ruling oligarchy to the people. Of course, there was a growing demand on the part of a small segment of the public for a share in the government. This politically conscious group consisted largely of the *samurai* who had not won their way into the oligarchy and had taken lesser posts in the new government or become business men. It also included other members of the business community who, as legal equals of the old *samurai* class, felt that they were entitled to a voice in the government. However, the oligarchy was not forced to make concessions to the public. It did so primarily because influential members of the ruling group had reached the conclusion from their study of Western political institutions that a constitution was essential to a strong westernized state, and that some form of parliamentary government was also a necessary part of the political machinery which helped make Western powers strong. . . .

The success of the carefully controlled revolution of the Meiji leaders was tremendous. In a few decades the oligarchs had made the strong Japan they wanted. They had no detailed plans when they started, but they did have a clear idea of the general objective, and this objective they had attained by firmly leading their people through a series of amazing reforms and changes.

Accustomed to severe feudal rule, the docile populace expected to be led. The oligarchs had no difficulty in controlling the people, and remained the masters of each new situation. Minor set-backs and endless personal quarrels occurred among the leaders, but all major issues turned out as they wished. Nothing got out of hand. Yet, in a country open to influences from all over the world, with an educated citizenry becoming aware of the ideas and ideals of other lands, strict control by a small oligarchy of the actions and thoughts of all the people became increasingly difficult.

It was in the intellectual field that new and divergent currents first made themselves felt. In the early days of Meiji, there had been many able young Japanese leaders who, while no less anxious than the Satsuma and Choshu *samurai* to make a new and better Japan, were not thinking primarily in terms of military strength. There were men like the young *samurai*, Fukuzawa Yukichi, who as a student of Dutch in the last years of the Tokugawa, had become aware of Western concepts, and later under the influence of American

ideals became a prolific writer, established a great newspaper, and founded an educational institution which was to become Keio University — one of the several great universities of modern Tokyo.

There were also foreigners in Japan, particularly the Christian missionaries, who came largely from America, and they helped found many of the early schools. Here they taught the Christian ideals of the West which, although tolerated by the early Meiji leaders, were quite at variance with their aims and beliefs. Christianity as an organized religion did not spread quickly in modern Japan, but it won a few hundred thousand converts who were drawn largely from the intellectual classes. Through them the ethics and ideals of Christianity had a much more profound influence on Japanese thought and life than one might assume from the fact that less than one per cent of the population became professing Christians.

The culture of the early Meiji period was a strange conglomeration of undigested borrowings from Western civilization mixed with many elements remaining intact from feudal times. In the late years of Meiji, however, the birth of a completely modern and yet indigenous culture was presaged by the appearance of an entirely new literature. . . . Its appearance toward the end of the Meiji period clearly indicated that, even while the oligarchy ruled, an intellectual class was growing up which was free of the feudal mentality inherited from the Tokugawa and was thinking in terms quite foreign to the oligarchs.

Side by side with the new intellectual class and to some degree merging with it was a second group, also developing opinions divergent from the ruling oligarchy. This group consisted of businessmen and financiers, who, although in large part made up of former *samurai* and Daimyo, tended to be more interested in taxes and profits than in military strength and colonial expansion.

The businessmen had joined with the lesser government officials excluded from the oligarchy in clamoring for a larger voice in the government, and the creation of the Diet in 1890 gave them a place in politics which they gradually improved. Political parties at first had centered completely around the old oligarchs, but as time passed the small ruling circle found it increasingly necessary to win the support of this new politically conscious public. Gradually the great financial and industrial interests began to take control of the parties, although the oligarchs still remained their nominal leaders. At the same time the electorate was expanded by lowering the tax requirement for voting. At the end of the First World War, the tax qualifications stood at only three yen, and the electorate had risen to 1,500,000, thus including the bulk of the middle classes, but not the peasantry and urban proletariat.

Despite these political gains of the middle classes and the appearance of new intellectual trends, Japan entered the First World War apparently under the firm control of a small oligarchy, and then, as the war ended and Japan entered the postwar world, it suddenly became evident that there was no longer a small, clear-cut ruling group, but instead, thousands of bureaucrats, military leaders, business men, and intellectuals, all contending for control of the government. There was even a growing demand that all classes be allowed to participate in politics. Within a few years it also became evident that the intellectual life and even the social patterns in the cities of Japan had become strongly westernized. A new Japanese culture . . . seemed to be emerging.

One reason for this rather sudden change was the disappearance of the original oligarchs. The Meiji emperor died in 1912, leaving the throne to his mentally deficient son, who ruled in name until 1926 under the reign title of Taisho. The Taisho emperor was incapable of participating in the direction of government, and in 1921 he had to relinquish even his ceremonial functions to his son, who became the Prince Regent. The death of the Meiji Emperor meant the disappearance of one of the greatest figures in the oligarchy and the elimination of the throne from Japanese politics, except as a symbol, and a tool for those in control of the government.

Ito, framer of the Constitution and four times Premier, had been assassinated by a Korean in 1909. Yamagata, father of the army and himself twice Premier, died in 1922. Two years later only one of the great "elder statesmen" of the Meiji period remained, Prince Saionji, the old court noble and perhaps the least typical member of the whole group.

Meanwhile, a new generation was coming into power. A majority of the generals, admirals, bureaucrats, businessmen, and intellectuals of the time had been born or at least had grown up since the "Restoration." These men, for the most part, were the sons of former *samurai* who had become army officers, government officials, or business men, but they, themselves, had never been *samurai*. No one group had the prestige or power of the old oligarchy, and on the whole they lacked the common background and singleness of purpose of the Meiji leaders.

Another significant factor was the First World War. It gave a tremendous impetus to commercial and industrial expansion, which helped make the business classes, and particularly the great commercial and industrial interests, increasingly important in Japanese life and politics. They became the heroes of a prosperous new Japan, and, as they spread their activities throughout the Far East, they began to overshadow the soldier and sailor as the front line fighters in Japan's expanding search for a place in the sun.

In addition, the overwhelming success of the Western democracies in the First World War strongly influenced Japanese thought. The most democratic Western powers, Great Britain, France, and the United States, had emerged victorious, and the least democratic, Germany, Russia, and Austro-Hungary, had collapsed completely. It seemed obvious that democracy made stronger states and was therefore superior to autocracy. This argument was convincing to the average Japanese. There was an upsurge of enthusiasm for democracy, which inevitably brought new powers and prestige to the Diet and the party politician.

[*There was an upsurge of enthusiasm for real democracy, and the business men of Japan, riding a wave of economic prosperity and responding to a popular demand for democratic government, became the dominant group in politics.—1946* EDITION]

With the disappearance of the old oligarchy and the growing influence of extra-governmental groups, the Diet and party system also proved to be handy mechanisms for the balancing of political forces. The great bureaucrats and high military and naval officers came closest, both in position and outlook, to being the heirs of the old oligarchy, but, lacking the unchallenged authority of their predecessors, they found it necessary to seek support through political coalitions in the Diet. The great business empires, which were coming to be known by the pejorative name of *zaibatsu,* found the Diet a convenient bargaining ground with the bureaucracy, while the parties were for them an effective tool for winning political power through the judicious use of financial aid. The smaller businessmen and rural landowners, who from the start had been the backbone of the political parties, naturally were committed to the support of parliamentary government, for that was their only means of exercising direct political power.

For these various reasons, then, the Diet and party system became the meeting ground for the plurality of forces which had grown out of the unity of earlier oligarchic rule. Professional bureaucrats, admirals, and generals, as well as representatives of the great *zaibatsu* firms, such as Mitsui and Mitsubishi, often dominated the leadership of the parties or even occupied the post of Premier, but for more than a decade after the First World War the Cabinets were largely party Cabinets, dependent upon an elected majority in the Diet. Corruption was rife, and the two major parties, the Seiyukai and the Kenseikai (renamed Minseito in 1927), were often the tools of strong individuals or powerful private interests. The Diet, however, had become the key instrument of government, and Japan had become the first non-Occidental land to make full use of democratic mechanisms, even though only a minority of the Japanese people had as yet found political expression through them.

[*Military officers, professional bureaucrats, and rural landowners all remained extremely influential, but the business men, particularly the representatives of great economic empires like Mitsui and Mitsubishi, dominated the post-war political parties, and these in turn controlled most of the Cabinets. Some of the Premiers were titled men, others were admirals without party connections; but for more than a decade after the First World War the Cabinets were largely party Cabinets, dependent for their authority upon party strength in the Diet. Thus, at last, the Diet became the key organ of government. Political parties often acted as tools of small but powerful private interests, and Japan had its full share and more of political corruption; but democracy, however imperfectly, was becoming the dominant force in Japanese politics.—1946* EDITION]

The new system of party government got its start as early as September 1918, when Hara, the Seiyukai leader, was the first commoner and the first professional politician of the new generation to become Premier. Actually the first Seiyukai leader to be Premier had been Prince Ito, but Ito, far from being the political product or agent of the party, had himself helped create it in 1900 in order to organize support in the Diet for his own policies. Hara, while high-handed in his efforts to dominate the party, was a product of party politics and dependent on Seiyukai support for his influence. Following his assassination by a fanatic in 1921, Cabinets came and went with bewildering rapidity, some backed by one economic empire or another, some more influenced than others by army and navy interests and more inclined to a strong foreign policy. But until the sudden collapse of party government in 1932, the general tendency was for the government to depend on party power in the Diet and to reflect the dominance of business interests over the other groups that constituted the ruling elements in Japan.

The Japanese businessmen of the 1920's, influenced by the philosophies of the victorious Western democracies, tended to look with disfavor on the high taxes required for large naval and military establishments. They were also inclined to believe that economic expansion — building up a great export trade and acquiring economic concessions abroad through diplomacy — was less costly and more profitable than colonial expansion by war and conquest. This seemed particularly true in China, the chief field for Japanese expansion. The Chinese, with a newly awakened sense of nationalism, were beginning to boycott foreign merchants whose governments were considered to be pursuing an aggressive policy against China. Consequently, military intervention in China cost the double price of lost markets and increased military expenditures.

Such attitudes, together with the prevalent internationalist sentiment of the postwar years, soon led to a reversal of the old policy of colonial expansion through military force.

[*The business men, acting through the government they now controlled, soon started a reversal of the old policy of colonial expansion through military force.*— 1946 EDITION]

In 1922, the Japanese withdrew from Siberia the last of their troops, which together with British and American forces had landed at Vladivostok, Russia's principal Far Eastern port, in 1918, shortly before Hara had come to power. On this expedition the Japanese had sent far more than their share of troops in an obvious effort to fish for possible rewards in the troubled waters of the Russian Revolution, but the new government considered the venture unprofitable and withdrew completely.

In the winter of 1921–22, at the Washington Conference, Japan joined the United States and the principal European powers in recognizing the territorial integrity of China and renouncing the generally accepted policy of cutting up the "Chinese melon." Japan also agreed with other members of the "Big Five" to limit their respective naval establishments. The ratio of capital ships was set at five for Great Britain and the United States, three for Japan, and 1.67 for France and Italy. This ratio, it was thought, would give Japan definite naval supremacy within her own waters but confine her fleet to the western Pacific.

This same winter, by a separate treaty with China, Japan restored to China the area around Kiaochow Bay and the economic concessions in contiguous parts of northern China once held by Germany. Japan also agreed to withdraw all her military forces from these areas. In 1925, the civilian government forced through a reduction of the standing army, and four of the twenty-one divisions were eliminated — a considerable cut in military strength and a saving to the tax-payer. Thus the Japanese businessmen called a halt to colonial expansion and asserted their right to limit and even to pare down the national military establishment.

From 1927 to 1929, the cabinet of Baron Tanaka, an army general and leader of the Seiyukai, reversed the trend away from militarism. He used Japanese forces in North China to block the northward advance of the new Chinese Nationalist government, but eventually he had to withdraw these troops. His successors returned to the dominant businessman's policy of conciliatory diplomacy with a view to further expansion of a lucrative export trade.

While a greatly enlarged ruling class of military leaders, bureaucrats, *zaibatsu* executives, and politicians representative of small business and rural landowner interests controlled the postwar parliamentarian regime, other classes were beginning to come on the political scene.

[*While a greatly enlarged ruling class of military leaders, bureaucrats, and business men, under the dominant influence of big business interests, controlled the democratic post-war regime, other classes were beginning to come on the political scene.*—1946 EDITION]

With the intelligentsia and underpaid office-workers in the van, city dwellers of lower economic status were waking to a new political consciousness. These men, too, belonged to the new generation and were the products of the new education. University professors, teachers, writers, doctors, lawyers, and office-workers, usually with from fourteen to eighteen years of formal education, were thoroughly conversant with the intellectual and political trends of the Western world. Even the city laborers, with their elementary education, could read the newspapers, which exposed them to influences from all quarters. The educated populace demanded a share in government, and with the democratic tide of the day, this demand could not be denied. In 1919, the electorate was doubled, increasing from 1,500,000 to 3,000,000; and in 1925, a universal manhood suffrage bill was passed, making a total electorate of 14,000,000 voters. Now the whole adult male population of Japan, peasants and city workers along with the middle and upper classes, could vote.

Since the lower classes, however, were politically untutored, they took little interest in politics. The peasantry seemed almost untouched by the strong democratic trends in the cities, and only a small element in the city proletariat, largely under the leadership of middle class intellectuals, expressed itself in political action. With the backing of white collar workers and some laborers, intellectuals founded liberal and left wing parties, such as the Social Democratic and the Labor-Farmer, and later the Social Mass Party, born of a union

of the two earlier parties. Even a Communist Party was organized, embracing a few radical thinkers and very small groups of laborers and peasants, but it was early liquidated by the thorough and ruthless Japanese police. Of the other parties, only the Social Mass made any impression in the Diet, and that was not until the 1930's, after the Diet had relapsed into relative insignificance.

Although the new parties were not too influential in practical politics, they were significant. During the 1920's, the city intellectuals and white collar workers became a strongly liberal group, not unlike the liberals in the United States who stood slightly left of center. In the 1930's, when the rest of Japan was disowning democracy and liberalism, and the businessmen were weakly surrendering leadership to the militarists, the intellectuals and white collar workers in the middle class districts of the large cities rolled up huge majorities for the few liberal politicians who were allowed to run for election.

The peasantry had not yet awakened to politics, and the urban proletariat was hardly strong; but without doubt the city workers were on their way to becoming a force in Japanese society and politics. Their medium of expression was more the labor union than the political party. Japanese labor unions, which had grown rapidly during the prosperous war years, were strong enough by 1919 to exert considerable pressure through strikes, and strikes became a definite part of the Japanese scene in the 1920's. By 1929, union membership had grown to well over 300,000 and promised to keep on growing. It seemed but a matter of time before the proletariat would join with city intellectuals and white collar workers to form a strong, possibly dominant political force in Japan. . . .

The leaders of the early Meiji period had transformed Japan into a strong military and industrial power, but the democratic political concepts, the broad intellectual life, and the liberal social trends which flowered spontaneously from the state they created were something they themselves could never have imagined or understood. The carefully controlled revolution of the Meiji period was developing into a runaway liberal movement of the urban middle classes. . . .

Ultra-nationalist and militarist sentiments from time to time found expression in political parties, but these essentially reactionary elements, with their inherent distrust of representative government, leaned more to direct action through private pressure groups and extra-legal cliques than to political action by means of the ballot-box. Ultra-nationalistic secret societies quite naturally developed as one of their major forms of political expression. Some of these exerted considerable influence on Japanese politics by terroristic activities and virulent propaganda directed against their opponents. The best known of these ultra-nationalistic secret societies was formed by anti-Russian propagandists who, believing that the Amur River in Siberia should be Japan's frontier, named their group the Amur Society. A literal translation into English has given us the very sinister sounding name of Black Dragon Society.

The reactionaries all tended to look to the armed forces as their idols and champions, for the army and navy were less tainted with the prevailing democratic views and businessman's ideals of the 1920's. The army and navy, furthermore, were the natural organs for the continued military expansion advocated by these reactionaries. The officer corps reciprocated by leaning heavily toward the expansionist and nationalistic views of the reactionaries. Older generals and admirals were often men of broad outlook, who from long and intimate association with business leaders had come to accept much of the business man's point of view, but the younger officers were mostly of a different breed.

The new officer caste was largely composed of sons of officers or of rural landowners, or sometimes even of peasants. Coming from such conservative backgrounds, they were given an even more conservative education. The army recruited most of its future officers at about the age of fourteen, and from that age on the young cadet was subjected to a narrow militaristic training which often made him incapable of understanding democratic concepts of government, or even the civilian mentality. Since these young officers were victims of over-indoctrination, it is not surprising that they increasingly found themselves in violent opposition to the trends of the time and completely out of sympathy with the more moderate and broadminded generals and admirals. . . .

Modern Japanese totalitarianism . . . was not merely an outgrowth of Japan's authoritarian past but was equally a product of the centralizing power of the modern economic and political machine. Modern communications as well as modern techniques of political and economic organization had given even the parliamentary government of the 1920's far greater control over the lives of the Japanese people than any emperor, Shogun, or Daimyo had ever exercised. Universal education, the newspapers, the radio, and, of course, universal military service had given those in power far greater control over men's minds than could have been dreamed of in earlier ages. Totalitarian patterns were certainly as natural an outgrowth of the Meiji modernization as liberal ideals and democratic institutions. It took time for these contrasting products of modernization to mature, and they emerged from the chrysalis of the controlled Meiji revolution at about the same time. . . .

These disturbing tendencies grew slowly and almost unnoticed during the 1920's; then in the early 1930's the blatant militarism, fanatical nationalism, and anti-liberal and anti-democratic prejudices of the younger army and navy officers and of other reactionary groups swept over Japan in a sudden reversal of the dominant trends of the preceding decade. The parliamentary coalition of the bureaucrats, big business, and the politicians, with more or less active support from the urban middle classes, had been the first successor of the Meiji oligarchy. Now it was pushed aside by the militarists, with the noisy backing of ultra-nationalistic societies and the tacit support of the rural population.

The exact time and speed of the reaction against liberalism and democracy were certainly influenced, if not determined, by outside forces, just as the rapid growth of liberal tendencies had been fostered by the external factor of the First World War. For one thing, the world-wide disillusionment with democracy, which followed soon after and helped to create fascist totalitarian regimes elsewhere, did not go unnoticed by the Japanese. Many of them were impressed by the vaunted "superiority" of totalitarian governments and their points of agreement with traditional Japanese concepts of authoritarian rule.

Another outside influence was the world-wide depression of 1929 and the resultant collapse of international trade. . . .

There was a gradual swing of popular support to the military expansionists. As these same groups also stood for authoritarian rule within Japan, much of the support for imperialist aggrandizement abroad readily became popular backing for the attack on democratic institutions at home. The incipient Japanese totalitarians, however, did not wait until growing popular support should bring them victory at the polls. That might never have come, and, in any case, it was a means to power which they, as a matter of principle, repudiated. Instead they began a direct, frontal attack on liberal beliefs and democratic institutions. They had no well-defined philosophy or central, conspiratorial organization, such as had helped the German Nazis and Russian Communists to win power. The attack was made piecemeal by individuals or small organizations, but it was almost as effective as the better coordinated efforts of the totalitarians in Europe.

Scores of small groups of fanatical nationalists stirred up popular support for the militarists and hacked away at the foundations of parliamentary government. Occasionally young hotheads were inspired by their rabid elders to commit political assassinations, which not only eliminated their unfortunate victims but, through intimidation, silenced large numbers of other potential opponents. Most important of all, the army on its own authority embroiled Japan in foreign wars of conquest, which, while forcing the nation back to the strategy of military conquest, also aroused the nationalistic emotions of the people and, thus, won their support for the authoritarian as well as the imperialist aims of the militarists.

The ease with which the Japanese totalitarians stifled the growth of democracy in Japan illustrated the obvious fact that the roots of liberalism were still shallow. It also revealed certain specific weaknesses in the democratic mechanism, attributable to its authoritarian background and haphazard growth.

One basic flaw in the whole Japanese political system had been deliberately fashioned by the Meiji oligarchs and carefully preserved by the parliamentary groups of the 1920's until it contributed to their own undoing. This was the mystic position of the emperor as a demi-god whose personal will, in theory, took precedence over all law. The Meiji leaders, who had come to power by championing the right of the emperor to rule, had created and fostered this tradition, since it gave them, as the men who surrounded the throne and spoke for the emperor, far greater authority over the people than they could have achieved otherwise. By building up an elaborate state cult of Shinto, centered on the person of the emperor and the imperial line, and by indoctrinating school children with fanatical devotion to the emperor and blind faith in all statements said to represent his will, they secured for themselves the unquestioning loyalty and obedience of the people. The parliamentary leaders who succeeded to power chose to perpetuate this system, for it seemed to give them, too, an unassailable position of authority as spokesmen for the emperor. Consequently, they permitted the wildest sort of utterances by members of the lunatic fringe of ultra-nationalists and militarists, because they were couched in terms of devotion to the emperor; but they vigorously and ruthlessly suppressed all radical thinkers who challenged the validity of the emperor concept.

In 1925, the same year in which universal manhood suffrage was adopted, the Diet passed a new Peace Preservation Law, further limiting the rights of free speech and free political action. Under the new law the government became increasingly involved in efforts to stamp out "dangerous thoughts." Any thought was considered dangerous which questioned the position of the emperor or challenged other basic political or economic beliefs of the ruling groups. Although anti-capitalist prejudices were perhaps most prevalent in extreme militaristic circles, the businessmen and bureaucrats were far more afraid of Marxist intellectuals, and the early victims of this thought purge were largely students of liberal or radical tendencies. The embryo communist movement was completely crushed, and many students who had nothing more than vague radical leanings were thrown into prison and forced to recant their "dangerous thoughts."

The parliamentary leaders made their fatal error in failing to see that the reactionary ultra-nationalists and militarists presented the most immediate threat to their continued supremacy. These groups neatly turned the tables on the civil government by claiming that they, not the government, represented the true imperial will. The claim in the case of the army had a certain validity, for in theory the armed forces were the personal army and navy of the emperor, enjoying under him a status of equality with the civil government and therefore equally qualified to speak for him. Profiting from this break in the solid front of government authority and taking advantage of tacit army approval, individual extremists were able to go even

further in claiming imperial sanction for their personal views and deeds. Acts of aggression abroad and, at home, acts of civil disobedience, political murders, and open mutiny were all justified as being in accord with the true will of the emperor, whose views, it was claimed, were misrepresented by the corrupt politicians around the throne.

Confronted with this monstrous perversion of their own policy, the weak-kneed parliamentarians failed to take drastic measures or even to stand firm and united. Instead, they all but openly admitted the justice of the charge by remaining silent and by compromising with their attackers. The more liberal elements in the urban population, while dismayed, were too weak politically and, for the most part, too timorous to fight back. The general rural and small-town population accepted these acts of supposed devotion to imperial will at their face value and created an atmosphere so sympathetic to political assassins and other extremists that such offenders were usually given only absurdly light punishment.

The theory of the imperial will, thus, was a fatal flaw in Japan's political structure, but the militarists could not have exploited it so successfully if the armed forces had not in practice enjoyed considerable independence of public control and autonomy within the government. This was another serious constitutional flaw. Diet control over the Cabinet was never fully established even in the 1920's, because the Diet never won full control over the purse strings. If the budget were rejected by the Diet, the Cabinet had the right to continue in force the budget of the preceding year.

The army and navy, moreover, maintained considerable independence of the Cabinet by insisting that the army and navy ministers be active officers of high rank and therefore subject to military discipline and available for service in the Cabinet only with army and navy approval. This ruling, first made in 1895 and given imperial sanction five years later, permitted the armed forces to destroy Cabinets or prevent undesirable leaders from taking the premiership simply by refusing to let any qualified officers accept portfolios in the government. The use of this stratagem as early as 1912 and 1914 indicates the growing divergence in opinion between military and civil officials even at that early date. This ruling was subsequently dropped, only to be revived in 1936, when it proved a valuable asset to the militarists in their bid for power. The armed forces, thus, had not only established their independence of the civil government but had rewon a virtual veto power over the Cabinet. The way was open for any action the army wished to take.

Throughout the 1920's certain high government officials had advocated colonial expansion and a strong military policy. There was, for example, Baron General Tanaka, who intervened in the Chinese civil war in 1928. Although the so-called Tanaka Memorial, a purported secret government document recommending a policy of conquest and empire in East Asia, is no longer generally accepted as an authentic document, views such as it expressed were advanced by many officials at the time. These men, however, had tried to win acceptance of their program by normal political procedures; moreover they had been willing to accept defeat when overruled by other groups in the parliamentary coalition.

The turning point between the more liberal 1920's and the reactionary 1930's came in 1931, when certain military forces, without the approval or knowledge of the civil government, started their own war of territorial aggrandizement. In September, Japanese army units stationed in Manchuria to protect the great South Manchurian Railway and other Japanese interests, embarked upon the conquest of all Manchuria on the flimsy pretext that Chinese troops had tried to blow up the railway. Within a few months, Manchuria had been overrun. Meanwhile, Japanese naval forces had been landed at Shanghai

in central China. After a sanguinary fight, they seized the Chinese portions of this key city and some surrounding territory. Early in 1932, Manchuria was made into the puppet state of "Manchukuo." . . .

There could be no doubt that the Japanese army in Manchuria had been eminently successful. . . .

The people as a whole accepted this act of unauthorized and certainly unjustified warfare with whole-hearted admiration. Many businessmen and bureaucrats, instead of denouncing the militarists for acting against the will of the government and therefore against the will of the emperor as interpreted by the government, happily accepted this expansion of the national domain and attempted to justify the acts of the military before a critical world public. The Japanese government, in fact, steadfastly maintained the fiction that there had been no war and called the whole conquest of Manchuria simply the "Manchurian incident."

Meanwhile, other military extremists at home had brought a sudden end to party rule by another form of direct action — political assassination. On May 15, 1932, a group of young naval officers and army cadets, claiming that they were attempting to free the emperor from evil advisers, assassinated Premier Inukai, a professional politician and the head of the majority Seiyukai Party. The army, profiting from this incident, demanded the end of party Cabinets, and the bureaucrats, while condemning the act of violence, tacitly accepted it as judgment against party government. Viscount Admiral Saito, a professional naval man of moderate leanings, was chosen to be the Premier of a compromise "National Government," in which the Cabinet was made up of a central bloc of professional bureaucrats, with other contingents from the political parties and the armed forces balancing each other.

Such compromise governments became typical of the rest of the 1930's. The military element in succeeding Cabinets tended to grow and party representatives slowly dwindled in number, but the professional bureaucrats retained the central and, theoretically, the dominant position throughout the decade. However, the militarists definitely took the lead in creating new policies of government. With the success of their Manchurian venture assured and with the support of sporadic acts of terrorism by individual extremists, they forced as much of their program as they could on the compromise governments.

By simply refusing to recognize the authority of the Diet over the Cabinet, the militarists robbed the Diet of one power after another, and by the end of the decade they had reduced it to little more than an impotent and very timorous debating society. They did not dare to do away with the Diet entirely, because in theory it had been a gift from the Meiji Emperor, but they made it meaningless as a parliament. . . .

The militarists also sanctioned and encouraged a veritable witchhunt for all persons whose slightest word or deed could be construed to be lèse majesté. Liberal educators were forced to resign their academic positions on the grounds that they had handled the Imperial Rescript on Education improperly, and leading statesmen were driven out of political life because of some unfortunate historical allusion involving an emperor. Even the two great Imperial Universities at Tokyo and Kyoto, which had always enjoyed great prestige and considerable academic freedom, were condemned for harboring "red" professors and were subjected to purges. In 1933 a group of liberal professors was forced out of the Law Department of Kyoto Imperial University, and two years later Professor Minobe of Tokyo, a leading authority on constitutional law and a member of the House of Peers, was forced into dishonorable retirement because he had described the emperor as an "organ" of the state. Social scientists, liberal educators, and moderate politicians soon learned to remain silent if they could not express themselves in the mystical terms of ultra-nationalism and abject devotion to the emperor.

The ultra-nationalists and militarists made skillful though possibly unconscious use of the smear technique. They exploited to the full each example of parliamentary corruption, making even minor incidents into major scandals which were thought to discredit all democratic government. Since the zaibatsu interests did exert an undue influence over the political parties, it was not hard to turn the vague economic unrest of the peasantry and the more conscious distaste for capitalism shared by various other groups in Japan into a distrust of democracy. . . . Since both capitalism and democracy had developed under strong Occidental influence, it was not hard to convert the hitherto latent resentment of Western power and prestige into an animosity for the political and economic institutions derived in such large part from the West. . . .

A major reason for the weakness of the defense of parliamentary government in Japan was that many members of the parliamentary coalition had little faith in democracy as such and looked upon the Diet and party government merely as convenient mechanisms through which they could exert their own influence. Such groups were won over with relative ease to a new coalition of forces, which had little trouble in silencing the weak and inexperienced elements still committed to democracy. The transition from the parliamentary 1920's to the increasingly totalitarian 1930's, thus, came about through no political upheaval but rather through a small shift in the make-up of the forces which stood behind the government.

Even when party governments were in power, the professional politicians and the popular vote they represented constituted only one of the forces in the coalition. There were also the zaibatsu interests, with their great financial power. Most important of all, there were the civil bureaucrats, who enjoyed the prestige of government position and manipulated the mechanisms of government control. And finally, but by no means least, there were the military bureaucrats, the army and navy officers, forming a strong deterrent drag, if not a positive pull, on the politically conservative side. The center of political gravity rested perhaps somewhere between the civil bureaucrats and the party politicians. Only a small shift of the center of gravity to a point somewhere between the civil and military bureaucrats spelled the end of parliamentary government. . . .

The story might have been different if the politicians had received strong vocal support from the public they represented. The political parties had always been dominated by the small businessmen and rural landowners. By the 1920's the white-collar urban vote was beginning to exert a noticeable pull toward the left, but the peasantry and urban labor still had no clear political influence. The parties, thus, represented primarily a conservative, propertied group, which fell easy prey to nationalistic slogans and the patriotic fever of war times. As a result, they allowed themselves to be stripped of their parliamentary means of political expression with hardly a murmur of protest. In 1940 the parties meekly voted themselves out of existence and merged in the Imperial Rule Assistance Association. This organization, which had been designed to be a totalitarian political party, proved to be stillborn. However, with the old parties now gone, the Cabinet had nothing more to fear from the Diet or the voting public it represented, except for an occasional pointed question from some exceptionally hardy politician left over from an earlier age.

Since the less conservative urban public had only been on the fringes of the parliamentary coalition, it was disposed of with even greater ease. Labor's start toward self-expression through union organization was quickly squelched, and the Social Mass Party of the city white-collar workers, swayed by the dominant currents of the day, itself developed certain fascist leanings before leading the procession of parties into the political morgue of the Imperial Rule Assistance Association. Many liberal intellectuals remained in determined opposition to developments at home and abroad, but they were forced to limit their activities to veiled criticisms which had no immediate political influence.

While the voting public was being squeezed out of the governmental coalition, the *zaibatsu* interests were making a practical compromise with the anti-capitalistic militarists. The *zaibatsu* had stood behind the parties, but they had also stood behind a strong centralized government and rigid police control of the people. They were no more committed to parliamentary government than to autocracy. Business meant far more to them than political principles. The vast new field for economic exploitation provided by the militarists in Manchuria became to a large extent the special domain of a newly risen group of *zaibatsu*, but the wars and rearmament programs of the militarists led to a rapid development of heavy industry and of certain other specialized war industries to the benefit of all the big industrialists. The average *zaibatsu* executive remained afraid of the risks and expense of a major war, but he was not averse to cooperating with the militarists in minor colonial ventures and in the profits of building an empire. The militarists for their part, while initially suspicious or openly hostile toward big business and capitalism in general, discovered early in their Manchurian venture that they could not fully exploit the empire they were conquering or develop the war industries they needed without the full and willing cooperation of big business.

The coalition of the military with the *zaibatsu* interests was perhaps nothing more than a marriage of convenience, but it was nevertheless a successful working arrangement. And as time went on, it began to be something more. *Zaibatsu* firms, such as Mitsui and Mitsubishi, in many respects represented monopoly capitalism, but at the same time, because of their very size, they made the transition to a state-controlled economy easier than it would otherwise have been. In preparation for the unspecified "national crisis" of the militarists, the government increasingly assumed direction over broad segments of industry and commerce, and the great *zaibatsu* combines, which were coming to be run by professional managers rather than by their owners, were convenient units of governmental control. The pressures of war hastened the growth of such controls, and the *zaibatsu* combines tended more and more to become economic branches of the state. Japan appeared to be taking the first steps toward a curious sort of state socialism, born of *zaibatsu* capitalism and sired by militaristic authoritarianism.

The civil bureaucrats, unlike the business interests, had not found parliamentary government a new means of political self-expression but had looked upon it rather as a dangerous challenge to their own power. They had compromised with the democratic upsurge of the 1920's, but in doing so they had fancied themselves as guiding rather than yielding to it. One of the weapons they had developed to insure that democracy could be kept under control had been the army, which, with the police, could be counted on, if necessary to support the government against the people. Now the bureaucrats, with little regret over the collapse of democratic forms of government, attempted to ride the new forces of militarism and ultra-nationalism, and again they imagined themselves as compromising with these pressures the better to guide them.

Throughout the 1930's the bureaucrats kept up the appearance of being in the political saddle, balancing the party politicians and big business interests against the militarists; but as the politicians and big business interests delined in power, it was more and more evident that the militarists, if not in the saddle, were at least leading the horse. All the bureaucrats could do was to exert a restraining influence on them. The bureaucrats were in no sense liberals, but they were at least moderates. Some even believed in parliamentary forms of government; most of them believed in the capitalist system, which the more extreme militarists were ready to discard; and many of them were undoubtedly apprehensive about the ultimate outcome of the aggressive foreign policy the militarists were pursuing.

THE PEOPLE'S RIGHTS MOVEMENT, THE DIET, AND THE EARLY PARTIES

The Importance of the Early Political Parties — A Contemporary View (1906)

ITAGAKI TAISUKE, ŌKUMA SHIGENOBU, AND UKITA KAZUTAMI

Dr. Reischauer's sketch of the development of modern Japan does not discuss the role of the leaders of the opponents of the Meiji government in the events leading up to the creation of the Diet in 1890. But in order to discover what democratic tendencies existed we have to focus attention on the origin of the political parties, led by Itagaki, Ōkuma, and others who became opponents of those in power and hoped to gain power themselves partly through the mobilization of "public opinion" in the context of Japan of the 1870's and 1880's.

Both Itagaki of the Tosa clan and Ōkuma of Hizen had taken part in the overthrow of the Tokugawa regime in concert with the Satsuma and Chōshū clans. They were also counted among the most capable organizers of the Meiji government. But Itagaki criticized his colleagues for concentrating too many powers in the hands of the central government and in protest resigned from the administration for the second time in 1876. Ōkuma remained in the government until 1881, when he was forced out partly over his view that a parliament should be established immediately and that "constitutional government is party government." He was feared by the other oligarchs, not only for his views but also for his ability and ambition. Ōkuma was supported by the more liberal-minded young intellectuals of samurai background and it was not out of keeping with his character that he became the founder of Waseda University in Tōkyō which remains to this day a fountainhead of the "opinion makers" of Japanese political and social life.

The following selection was actually written by Professor Ukita of Waseda but was intended to represent the views of Itagaki and Ōkuma just after the Russo-Japanese War of 1904–5. As such, the advice herein proferred to the political parties is extremely interesting for revealing what they thought the functions of parties to be: limiting centralized power, proposing reforms, recruiting new leadership, reconciling through representation various social classes and unifying the people behind the government on foreign policy. Their demands for "political liberty" turn out to be quite moderate. They appear to be satisfied with the parliamentary institutions as set out in the Meiji Constitution of 1889 and place their hope for the future on the eventual maturation of the political parties.

From Shigenobu Ōkuma, compiler, *Fifty Years of New Japan* (*Kaikoku Gojūnen Shi*) Vol. I (London, 1909), pp. 185–193.

THE history of Japanese political parties . . . may be divided into four periods. The first began with the movement inaugurated by Itagaki, Soyéshima, Gotō, and Etō in 1874 by the presentation of a memorial for the establishment of a popularly elected legislative assembly, and closed with the withdrawal of Ōkuma from the Government in 1881. It was during this period that political parties had their origin. Though as yet no organized body existed, still the fact that there was a party in unorganized form, whose leader was Itagaki, cannot be questioned. The second period began with the secession of Count Ōkuma, and the issue of an Imperial decree promising the establishment of a Diet in 1890. This was followed by the Government's instruction to Itō and other officials to formulate the Constitution. During this period political parties reached the stage of organized bodies. They were subjected to severe Government persecution, and the "Jiyūtō" [or Liberal Party] was for a time forced to dissolve, although it was recognized just before the opening of the first Diet and became a nucleus for the combination of the Opposition. During the third period, which commenced with the opening of the Diet in 1890, the Government fought bitterly against the combined forces of the "Jiyūtō" and the "Kaishintō" [or Reform Party]. Strenuous efforts made by the Cabinet to control the Diet, by dissolving it and then by interfering with the elections, proved futile, and the opposition parties always commanded a majority in the Lower House. The relations of the Government to the Diet were in a most perplexing condition, when they were suddenly relieved by the war with China [1894–95]. Thereafter, the Government recognized the defeat of its attempt to suppress political parties, and the political parties also began to realize the disadvantage of their being always in opposition to the Government. The "Jiyūtō" and then the "Kaishintō" allied themselves with the Government, but finding the result unsatisfactory, both coalesced and jointly formed a party Cabinet [1898], which failed owing to a lack of unity. These successive events demonstrated the impossibility of maintaining the Government without the help of political parties, on the one hand, and the immaturity of the parties to establish their own Cabinet, on the other.

The fourth period commenced with the dissolution of the Ōkuma-Itagaki Cabinet and the organization of the second Yamagata Ministry in 1898, and runs into a future whose termination is as yet invisible to us. This is the period during which the bureaucratic Government and one of the parties, having effected a compromise, are working together in the administration of national affairs. The formation of the "Séiyūkai" Cabinet under Itō seemed for a time to indicate the success of party government, but when it fell without any attack from external foes, the unripeness of political parties to take upon themselves the responsibility of Government was again proved. The successive failures of party Cabinets under Ōkuma and Itō may not be final, but may be signs of tentative movements and an advance towards ultimate success. The "Kenséitō" Cabinet [of 1898], formed when the amalgamation of the "Shimpotō" [or Progressives] and the "Jiyūtō" had not yet matured, was a temporary union of two bodies having different heads and members. What Napoleon said about one bad general being better than two good ones is also true in the case of political parties. It was not surprising, therefore, to see a dissolution of the "Séiyūkai" Cabinet [in 1901] under the conditions of a conflict between the members of the former "Jiyūtō" and the immediate associates of Marquis Itō. It was a case of an organization having one head but various limbs actuated by irreconcilable feelings and interests. These experiences do not at all demonstrate the hopelessness of party government, but simply show the difficulty of maintaining a union of two parties, and the weakness of a coalition Cabinet based upon such a union.

Theoretically speaking, political parties

should not necessarily be limited to two, but there should be several different parties, according to the nature of the problems and questions presented. A mixed Cabinet under such circumstances may be considered as the form of government best adapted to represent popular opinions and sentiments. Notwithstanding these theoretical views, study of the English and American systems of Government, where party politics have been tried so long, points to a tendency to produce two great parties as a result of the constant struggle for existence, in which smaller parties are defeated and pass out of existence or are absorbed into larger ones. On the other hand, the influence and strength of political parties on the European Continent are very feeble where the above-mentioned tendency is not known, and where there are many small parties in existence. It is not on account of the truth of any political theory that two great political parties are produced in England and America; it is simply a natural consequence of party politics and the struggle for supremacy. Therefore, there have been many instances in which a political or social question changed the existing conditions, and split up a powerful party into fragments, some of which became independent, while others joined the opposite party and formed a mixed Cabinet. In such cases we no longer see a strong Cabinet which can maintain the unity and continuity characteristic of one based upon a large and harmonious single party. It is then the natural sequence of events that a similar tendency towards the gradual formation of two large parties should prevail in this country.

The peculiarity of our political parties in general is that they are all moderate in principles and very gradual in their progress. There is a conservative party, but no reactionary one. There is a progressive, but no extreme radical or revolutionist party. It is true that the *"Jiyūtō"* at first gave some indication of becoming a revolutionary party, but that phase has disappeared with the establishment of constitutional government. The *"Shimpotō"* is radi-

cal in some respects, but its radicalism is limited to questions concerning foreign affairs or ministerial responsibility; on all other matters it maintains a dilatory and conservative attitude. The *"Séiyūkai"* has been, above all, mild and moderate both in domestic and foreign politics. As for the *"Téikokutō,"* formerly known as the *"Kokumin Kyōkai"* and now as the *"Daidō* Club,"* which holds the balance of power between the two great parties, it may be said that it is somewhat more conservative in domestic politics than the *"Séiyūkai,"* but that it stands on the same level with the *"Shimpotō"* in regard to foreign politics, and has always advocated the expansion of armaments. It now holds a very feeble position among the parties. Naturally, a party with the almost meaningless name of *"Kokumin Kyōkai"* (National Association) or *"Téikokutō"* (Imperialists) grows weaker and feebler, as is actually the case. Such a party has no particular principle to uphold and cannot succeed in a country like ours, where there is perfect unity among the people and where there is not a single element of racial or sectional discord. After all, unless there come a change in social conditions, with the consequent rise of a labour or socialist party, it is reasonable to suppose that the present political situation will remain unchanged.

In order to establish a form of government of which the people of the Orient had never dreamed, and to obtain rights and liberties for people the majority of whom had no notion about such things, the political parties of our country hoisted high the flag of liberty and constitutional government and assailed the fortress of clan bureaucratic despotism with manly courage. The time has been too short since these parties were formed to furnish the people with an opportunity for the training and discipline necessary in political movements and organizations. Hence the success attained by the parties in establishing constitutional government is nothing short of marvellous. That they could not hold the reins of power in their own hands after they obtained the coveted prize, that they could not secure the sympathy and support of a people habitually indifferent to party politics, and that they had to contend more than once with the too strong opposition of conservative associations, must be regarded as inevitable results where a party system is not yet firmly established. But, when it is remembered that the political parties remedied the evils of clan oligarchy by their opposition and contributed materially towards many political reforms and advancements, thus rendering good service to the people, we can easily see that the benefits conferred by political parties have more than counterbalanced their defects and failures. If the political parties had not arisen in 1873–74, and if their activities had not increased after 1877, there would not have been in 1890 the establishment of constitutional government. If the old system of arbitrary government still continued to exist, there would have been no means of checking it, and there would have been hindrances and obstructions to internal improvement. The wide barrier between the people and the Government, and also the sharp distinctions between various classes, would have remained more marked than it is now, making it hard to maintain the progress already accomplished, imperfect as it is. In particular, it would have been evidently impossible to realize such success at a time of external crisis as we obtained in the late two wars with China and Russia through the united effort of the whole nation. Therefore, although there are many things to be regretted, such as the ineffectiveness of political parties, the imperfection of the Diet, the disorganized condition of public affairs, the backward tendency of the conservative elements, and many other cognate instances, we must wait, practise patience, and not expect too much in our passionate zeal. But, to hold that the old system of government is better because of the evils which prevail under the new, and to overlook the benefit of constitutional government and the merit of political parties, must be regarded as an unfair judgment of

biased men. Without political parties it is hopeless to see the full operation of the representative system and to secure the benefits of constitutional government. Viewing the matter from this standpoint, the nation must hope for the progress and development of political parties. The first immediate duty of a political party is to deepen and broaden its basis among the people. It must educate the people in political affairs, so that they can sympathize with and become strong supporters of the party's programme. It must extend the suffrage, strengthen the power and enlarge the sphere of public opinion, in order to firmly and permanently establish the foundations of political parties, and train the people so that they may be able to understand the nature of the topics of the day, and to adopt the principles or policy of the party which they approve. Again, it is the duty of a political party to advocate the reform and improvement of internal administration, and thereby promote the progress of society. Hitherto, the parties opposing the Government have, time and again, contended with it on issues relating to foreign politics. This is to fight on ground advantageous to the enemy, for the facts of foreign politics are usually kept secret, so that the gist of the affair is unknown to the public until the critical moment is past. It cannot, therefore, be a wise step for political parties to make such a matter an issue between them and the Government. The country's foreign policy must be established upon some fixed national principle, and in execution of that policy great tact, discretion, and prudence must be observed. Who knows but there may be an irretrievable mistake on the part of the Government, if it follows popular sentiment with regard to foreign relations, however clamorous the cry may be? There is therefore wisdom on the part of our people, since they rely more upon the ability of the Government than they trust the capacity of political parties to judge rightly on foreign affairs.

Political parties should therefore make

domestic questions, rather than foreign policy, a subject of contention with the Government, thus educating the people politically, appealing to their sympathy for the principle at stake, and giving them an opportunity to pass an opinion on it. The majority of the people are certainly not intelligent; hence to awaken their sympathy, to secure their support, and finally to create public opinion by spreading the views of a small body of intelligent men, requires no little patient labour and training. If we observe carefully the present political, social, and economical conditions of our nation, there is clearly a wide field for the future activity of political parties. The central Government, with its strongly concentrated powers, is harassing everything, suppressing the spirit of the people for autonomy, and barring the development of constitutional institutions. Reform on these points should be made an issue by the political parties opposed to the Government. Again, our educational system sets education and religion entirely apart, giving unparalleled advantages for the management of schools, which cannot be found in Occidental countries; but in spite of this, the evil tendencies of centralized government manifest themselves here also; the independent spirit is lacking in educators, and the system abounds in formalities, no part having any vital power unless set in motion by the central authorities, nor is the system well fitted to develop men of talent and to discipline a great nation. These are timely questions on which the political parties should advertise their opinions and arouse public sentiment. As a result of social development the gulf between the rich and the poor is widening; and the progress of industry, which requires vast capital, produces more wealth, but has a tendency to cramp the freedom of men. There are, besides, many other questions of a local nature which demand solution by intelligent people. Should the political parties turn their attention towards them, there can be no doubt that there will be a prompt and active response on the part of the people.

The history of political parties is the history of constitutional government in Japan. It was the political parties who first created the public demand for the establishment of a national assembly and hastened the enactment of the Constitution, and later, commanding a majority in the Diet, forced the Government to act constitutionally, while the people in general were as yet indifferent to the right of participation in political affairs. In some respects the significance of political parties is greater in Japan than in England. The political parties in England arose several hundred years after Parliament had come into existence. Before the parties became of any use to the nation, Parliament existed as an essentially important organ and rendered effective services to the public. Not so in our country. Here the political parties antedated the Constitution and the Diet, the former being the motive power which produced the latter. In England the Parliament was prior to the political parties, and was one of the causes which produced them. But in Japan the political parties arose before the Diet came into existence, and were the chief causes which produced the Diet. If the two large parties — the *"Séiyūkai"* and the *"Shimpotō"* — were taken out of the Diet, there would be no life or vitality in the latter. Therefore, the repeated failures of party Cabinets may be said to be nothing but a step towards success in future years, when they can have the support and confidence of the people. Unfortunately, the tendency of all political parties in every country is to resort to any means, regardless of moral worth, in order to defeat their opponent, and thus to obtain their immediate end. We here in Japan view with much regret how unworthy of our respect are some individual members of the political parties. But when we consider their past successes and their future prospects, there can be but one opinion in regard to our political parties as an indispensable element of our constitutional government.

Limitations on the Early Democratic Movement
Due to its Agrarian Character

E. HERBERT NORMAN

If the movement that pressed for constitutional government was simply a power play by those leaders who had been squeezed out of the Meiji government during the first dozen years of its struggle for survival, would not it be difficult to argue that a democratic potential really existed in Meiji Japan? Nevertheless, whatever the personal motives of men like Itagaki and Ōkuma, they were able to mobilize social forces that made progressive demands on the government. This distinguished them from the other important Restoration leader who also became disgruntled and withdrew from the government, Saigō Takamori. Saigō came to represent those forces that opposed the government's program of modernization and longed for the restoration of feudal privilege. Restoring to arms, they rose in rebellion but were crushed in 1877. The social forces behind Itagaki and Ōkuma were of a different nature.

Dr. Norman, the Canadian diplomat who distinguished himself as a scholar on modern Japanese history, wrote the pioneer study in English on the forces behind the *jiyū minken undō* of the 1870's and 1880's which has been variously translated as the "freedom and people's rights movement" or the "liberal," "democratic," "popular," or "populist" movement. Well versed in the Japanese language, he drew on the scholarship of the Japanese intellectuals of the 1930's who had been heavily influenced by Marxism and who sought to explain why the class struggle had developed differently in Japan from the way it had in England, thus thwarting the rise of middle-class democracy.

According to Dr. Norman's analysis, the explanation lies in the social composition of the liberal movement in Japan. It was a rural, rather than an urban, movement, largely led by semientrepreneurial landlords. When the poorer tenant farmers agitated for rent reduction, the ardor of the local land-owners cooled. The movement broke up and the incipient Japanese middle class eventually settled for moderate political parties contending for limited rewards in an emasculated Diet. Dr. Norman saw future democratic possibilities in an extension of the suffrage for the lower house.

THE stormy politics of the first few years of the Meiji era up to 1877 were typical of any transitional period. The disappearance of the old, pure feudal classes, and the emergence of new social forces were marked by confusion and bitterness, by hopes aroused and too often disappointed. In the time of transition no clear-cut political divisions appear, only the hazy outline of tendencies which later were to become sharply defined as political parties with definite programs. . . . In the first six or seven years following the Restoration, peasant revolt reached an apex of violence and then gradually declined. The peasant movement was one of apparent contradictions, a mixture of reaction and radicalism which gave contemporary Japanese politics the ap-

From E. Herbert Norman, *Japan's Emergence as a Modern State: Political and Economic Problems of the Meiji Period* (New York, 1940), pp. 167–174, 178–185, 188–190, and 204–205. Reprinted by permission of the publishers, Institute of Pacific Relations, now distributed by the University of British Columbia, Publications Center, Vancouver, Canada.

pearance of a tapestry of intricate pattern showing no obvious design, but only a combination of vivid or somber concentrations of light and shade. When led by discontented *samurai,* this agrarian movement, which was the core of early Meiji political life in the broadest sense, represented a desire to return to the old order; when directed against usury, high rent and excessive taxation, it expressed a vague aspiration toward a fuller democracy. The first type of reactionary agrarian revolt, led by discontented elements and directed against the new régime, was gradually extinguished, so that after the suppression of the Satsuma Revolt (1877) it ceased to be important. Thereafter the agrarian movement branched off into three directions. First there was the agitation of the tenant for the reduction of rent. Second was the action of small landed proprietors who were menaced with dispossession and who struggled against usurers and aggrandizing landholders. The third type was the movement of landowners in general against the government policy of favoring the great mercantile and financial houses at the expense of the rural community. . . .

. . . [P]olitically the type of agrarian movement represented in the first and second categories was not so important in this period (1877–85). The third, which may be called a protest of landowning agriculturists against the favored position of the financial oligarchy, is the most significant historically. It is from this group that the cry "Liberty and People's Rights" arose most vociferously. Since these landowners were to become the standard-bearers of the constitutional movement, and since also they formed the background of the Liberal Party (*Jiyuto*), we may examine the features of this movement in some detail.

At first sight it might seem incongruous that landowners should form the core of the liberal movement. The word "landowner" at once brings to the mind of the Western reader the English squire and his deep-seated conservatism in all matters relating to society and politics. To explain the Japanese landowner's outlook we must hark back to analysis of Japanese tenant-landlord relations. . . .

The Japanese landlord collects rent while the tenant takes the entrepreneur's risks but not his profits. Thus the landlord is interested primarily in converting the rice or other agricultural produce collected as rent into money at the best possible rate. Hence his only concern is the current price of rice. His interest in turning agricultural products into commodities makes the Japanese landlord a small commercial capitalist who invests his money in land or in local domestic industries connected with the land, such as the making of *miso* (bean paste) and brewing of *sake,* or who becomes a rice-broker or small merchant of artificial fertilizer and the like. A foreigner who several years ago tramped far and wide over the Japanese countryside, making detailed notes on Japanese rural society, wrote in this connection, "When I drew attention to the fact that there (i.e. a village in Nagano prefecture) the manufacture of *sake* and soy seemed to be frequently in the hands of landowners, it was explained to me that formerly this was their industry exclusively." . . . Thus as the collector of an exorbitant rent he is a semi-feudal landlord, but he has also the other side, that of the commercial capitalist. It was this commercial capitalist side which drove the Japanese landlord into politics in the period of which we are speaking. This is seen in the active part played by landlord-manufacturers in forming the Liberal party, the *Jiyuto.* In 1880 a Council of *Sake*-Brewers (*Sakaya Kaigi*) was formed under the leadership of a certain Kojima Minoru and rapidly attracted to it great numbers of *sake*-brewers throughout the country. The government, which was then considering a program of naval expansion requiring increased taxation, proposed among other new methods of revenue increase a tax on *zoseki* (a yeast stone used in brewing). Immediately the *Sakaya Kaigi,* at the first conference of the *Jiyuto* in 1881, opposed this tax and raised the slogan "Freedom of Enterprise," worthy of the purest Manchester Liberal in 19th century England. The great popularity of this organization among village and town gentry alarmed the government, so that in December 1881 the council was dissolved at the order of the governor of Osaka-Fu. Despite the ban the brewers opened their session on a boat in the Yodogawa. The activity of this brewers' council attracted large numbers of landlord-manufacturers and small landlords with commercial interests into the *Jiyuto* and gave it the peculiar coloring described above, that is a Liberal party based on the landlord class. Thus his trading or manufacturing activities made of the Japanese landlord a modest Cobden, but his interests as landlord could make him intensely conservative.

The other concern of the landowning class in general was tax reduction. The government had reduced the land tax from 3 to 2½ per cent to conciliate the landowners and to dampen any sympathy they might entertain for the sporadic *samurai* revolts culminating in the Satsuma Revolt of 1877, which tax-reduction anticipated but did not prevent. Despite this conciliatory gesture, the landowning gentry felt that the weight of taxation was unduly heavy upon them. . . .

Accordingly, the landlords participated in the liberal movement, attacking the bureaucratic governing circle and its financial supporters as small commercial capitalists, interested primarily in rice-brokerage, in trading, in usury and in small local investments. It was this side which made them active champions of "Freedom and People's Rights" and "Freedom of Enterprise," and not the pure landlord side with its semi-feudal conservative character. The somber side of the landlord never disappeared even during the hey-day of liberalism, but lay dormant until later years when it completely overshadowed the "liberal" side. The point to note is that Japanese liberalism had its roots in the countryside, unlike English liberalism which was a movement of the cities especially of the city merchants

in opposition to the conservative landed gentry.

The theoretical leaders of the liberal movement were ex-*samurai,* chiefly from the former Tosa and Hizen clans which no longer shared equally in the fruits of office with Satsuma and Choshu. That many of these men were inspired by genuinely liberal ideals is not disputed; their later careers and sacrifices are sufficient testimony to their singleness of purpose. Nevertheless . . . the abolition of the clans had undermined the economic base of feudalism, leaving many discontented *samurai,* while the failure of the advocates for an expedition to Korea (*Seikan Ron*) had embittered others, and so these ex-*samurai* were drawn into the liberal movement merely because it was the *anti-government movement.* Thus individual place-seeking and jealousy of the *Sat-cho* [short for Satsuma and Chōshū clans'] monopoly acted as a stimulus for organizing the first political associations in Japan. It was natural that these ex-*samurai* in opposition to the government should become the acknowledged leaders of the movement which demanded a people's assembly. They enjoyed great prestige as members of the *shizoku* [or samurai] class, and above all as leaders in the Restoration of 1868. On this account some Japanese authorities have called them the heirs of the *Kinno* or *Sonno* Party (loyalists who fought against the *Bakufu* [or Tokugawa government]) and the true embodiment of the anti-feudal struggle.

But the impelling force of the liberal movement came from the great mass of small peasants, tenants and city poor who rallied to it urging the reduction of taxes, the establishment of representative institutions, even demanding representation in the liberal movement. It was difficult however for the peasants living in outlying, isolated villages to take active part in politics. It was only natural that the most active element in local politics should be the large landowners, while the national leadership tended to be in the hands of ex-

samurai or of a few large landlord merchants.

This widespread and loosely connected movement of small landowners and peasants under the leadership of former *samurai* and big landlord merchants took national form in the *Jiyuto* (Liberal Party) organized early in 1881. The quality of its leadership inevitably made the political philosophy of the *Jiyuto* a rather softened, conciliatory liberalism, a liberalism which strove primarily for democracy, for people's rights, for freedom of enterprise — all for the respectable classes. This is well brought out in the reply of the liberal leaders, Soyejima, Goto and Itagaki (who were to become the most active members of the *Jiyuto*), to Kato Hiroyuki's argument against representative government in Japan. "Now if this council chamber be established, we do not propose that the franchise should at once be made universal. We would only give it in the first instance to the *samurai* and the richer farmers and merchants, for it is they who produced the leaders of the Revolution of 1868."

Thus from its start Japanese liberalism as embodied in the *Jiyuto* was of a moderate, temporizing quality and later it was to change into its opposite, uncompromising conservatism, when the *Seiyukai* was formed from the ruins of the *Jiyuto* in 1900. We are not discussing here the extreme left-wing of the *Jiyuto*, which later took on almost a revolutionary coloring, but the basic political philosophy of the chief leaders of the *Jiyuto*. Despite any vagueness in its program, the *Jiyuto* before its split into local grouplets with a right and left wing, because of the enthusiastic backing it received from land-hungry tenants and debt-burdened peasant proprietors, had great *élan* and even revolutionary potentialities. For this reason, . . . the Government in its campaign of suppressing political parties launched its fiercest onslaught against the *Jiyuto*. . . .

[Earlier, however, when] the loosely-knit network of local debtors' parties and liberal societies was organized into national parties (particularly the *Jiyuto*), and when agitation for representative institutions became more violent, the Government decided again to make a concession. Accordingly in 1881 it promised the nation a Diet by the year 1889. But the Imperial Edict of October 12, 1881, promising the establishment of the national assembly, did not put an end to the demand for representative institutions, but added fuel to the democratic movement. This movement, as expressed in the growing popularity and power of political parties, was viewed by the Government with the greatest alarm and it took swift action by launching an attack against these two opposition liberal parties, the *Kaishinto* and *Jiyuto,* first by direct repression and secondly by splitting the liberal movement and winning over to its own camp some sections of the opposition. Having promised a Diet within nine years, the Government in 1882 passed new regulations in regard to meeting and association, which were far more severe and more rigorously enforced than the previous regulations. The most stringent repression, however, came only after the Government had succeeded in rendering the political movement ineffective either by winning over some of its leaders or by playing off the *Kaishinto* against the *Jiyuto,* and in this way removing some of the ablest political leaders from successful participation in the democratic movement.

Just at the time when the agitation for people's rights and representative institutions seemed to be sweeping victoriously over the country, indicating a crucial struggle in the near future with the Government, the members of the *Jiyuto* were amazed to learn suddenly late in 1882 that their most experienced leaders, Itagaki Taisuke and Goto Shojiro, were sailing for Europe to study Western political institutions at first hand. Rumors emanating from the *Kaishinto* and aired by the Tokyo-Yokohama *Mainichi Shimbun* insisted that the expenses for this trip were met by the Government. Although many of the *Jiyuto* members stoutly denied the charge that their leaders had been virtually bought off by the Government some of them . . . shortly withdrew from the party in protest. The truth was that the traveling expenses had been furnished by the Mitsui Company. . . . This dubious incident and its repercussions stung the *Jiyuto* into bitter recrimination against the *Kaishinto*. Okuma, the leader of the *Kaishinto*, was accused of acting as the political agent of the Mitsubishi Company and of pouring over-generous subsidies and grants into its coffers. . . . The upshot of this was that rather than combining to attack their common enemy, the absolutist clan government, the two opposition parties fell into the trap set for them by the Government, wrangled bitterly with each other and dissipated their energies in such a way as to discredit political parties and to strengthen the Government. Following its clever maneuvers in playing off one opposition party against another, the Government capped its campaign against the parties by the severe repression mentioned above. Faced with the alternative of carrying on the struggle by illegal methods or of bowing before the Government's will, most of the leaders of the liberal movement chose the latter course. In October 1884, the *Jiyuto* was voluntarily dissolved, while the *Kaishinto* preceded it by a year, dissolving in September 1883.

*   *   *

Even before the dissolution of the parties, with the press effectively muzzled and all political activity stringently suppressed, local branches of the political parties had energetically protested against government suppression and had even turned to insurrection as a means of achieving their end — the overthrow of the autocratic government. Many of the lesser leaders in the *Jiyuto*, angered and bewildered by what seemed to them the defection of their chiefs, often supported these ill-starred uprisings. The historical interest of these local incidents arises from the political and economic demands which motivated the rank and file of the liberal movement and

the resolution, however misplaced, with which these demands were backed in comparison to the tergiversations of the leaders. One of the shrewdest observers of Japanese national life, Fukuzawa Yukichi foresaw as early as 1881 the tendency for the rank and file in the liberal movement to display a violent impatience with government policy. In writing to Okuma, he says, "The *Minken Ron* (Advocacy of People's Rights) seems to be more and more favoring direct action. If it goes on in that direction, the antagonism between the government and people will become increasingly embittered, and in the end I fear it will mean unfortunate bloodshed."

Fukuzawa's forebodings were only too accurate. The first of these revolts broke out in 1882 in Fukushima prefecture. Indignation at the arbitrary action of the prefectural governor . . . in over-riding the prefectural assembly of Fukushima was the spark which kindled the uprising in that province. The leader was . . . a man of extreme views and resolute character. After the suppression of the revolt he and his associates were arrested and sentenced to imprisonment. Almost at the same time an uprising broke out in Takada of Niigata prefecture in which the leaders were accused of plotting to assassinate the government leaders. An insurrection occurred in Chichibu (Saitama prefecture) in 1884 in which the *Shakkinto* or local debtors' party played a leading role as did also a radical group from the local *Jiyuto*. These political leaders were alleged to have stirred up bad feeling among the peasantry and village poor against the local landlords, and when police arrived on the scene the peasants had resisted them forcibly. . . . [T]his Chichibu uprising symbolizes the great divide in the history of the *Jiyuto* or Liberal Party. We have already seen that leadership in this party was in the hands of landowners who were merchants or manufacturers as well; it was this commercial side of their nature which drew them into politics. However, as government repression became intensified to meet the mounting demand for greater democracy, these local branches, which were often in more radical hands than was the national leadership, stirred up such violent popular sentiment not only in favor of representative institutions but also for rent reduction that it terrified many of the more cautious leaders, bringing out the conservative landlord side of their nature, and thus made party dissolution by no means as unpalatable as it might otherwise have been. As one authority writes, "The *Jiyuto* and *Kaishinto* were more or less directly connected with the exhibition of violence in the provinces, though it is not likely that the leaders of either countenanced the measures adopted. To clear itself of the stigma of inciting to rebellion, the *Jiyuto* at a general meeting held on October 20, 1884, in Osaka, resolved to disband and wait for an opportunity when society will be prepared for its reconstitution."

After the dissolution of the *Jiyuto,* local uprisings such as those just described, usually led by the extremist followers of the *Jiyuto* or its offshoots, took on a most violent and bloody character. . . .

*   *   *

Thus ends the first chapter in the history of Japanese liberalism. Most instructive in this history is the evidence of the fundamental weakness in a liberalism which stemmed *from the countryside.* In other countries victorious liberalism, whether of the Independents or rather the London Presbyterians during the Cromwellian era or of revolutionary Paris, was essentially an urban movement which could draw on the immense financial power of the city merchant and could be propelled by the highly centralized political organization of the city masses. Above all, English and French liberalism, though led by wealthy merchants, lawyers or even country gentry, was reinforced by the presence in the metropolis of a large and comparatively articulate urban citizenry. This is, of course, equally true of 19th century English liberalism after the Reform Act of 1832,

when the Liberal Party drew its strength almost exclusively from the city classes. But in Japan a liberalism based on the countryside with its isolated villages, where local issues often absorbed the attention of the neighboring population to the exclusion of all else and where conditions differed widely from one locality to another, inevitably brought inner clashes and final failure. Furthermore the antagonism between the landlord leadership of the *Jiyuto* and the rank and file peasant following was bound to force a split in the party. We have seen how this leadership of the *Jiyuto* succumbed more easily to the government offensive after the startling incidents described above, when peasants voiced among other cries the demand for rent reduction. Deprived of all central leadership, the local branches of the *Jiyuto* under various names and for various local issues often resorted to violence in order to weaken the grip of government repression. These attempts were too scattered and sporadic, in a word *too local in character* both geographically and politically, to be crowned with even partial success. The government won out all along the line, thanks to the unity of the ruling bureaucracy and its autocratic methods on the one hand, and to the disunity and confusion of the opposition on the other.

The *Jiyuto* was reconstituted again with the opening of the Diet in 1890. But the series of successive splits by which the most radical groups within it had been gradually sloughed off, and the very high property qualifications for the electorate (payment of at least fifteen yen in direct national taxes) made the reformed *Jiyuto* a chastened and moderate party. Its transformation through various intermediate stages into the *Seiyukai* (1900), the party of the landlords, indicates the triumph of that semi-feudal landlord aspect in the leadership of the original *Jiyuto*.

*   *   *

Liberalism did not die with the dissolution of the political parties in 1883–4.

Nevertheless, after that first flush of political enthusiasm and fruitless energy it was to become a still more restrained and compromising movement. We have not the time here to trace the quick shifts and ephemeral coalitions of the various liberal factions led by Itagaki and Okuma; but while these factions intrigued for some share in the rewards of office, the government quietly went on strengthening its defenses against the sort of storm which swept the country from 1880–4. It also effected much needed administrative reforms which gave it greater flexibility and efficiency. The most energetic spirit in this government activity was Ito Hirobumi, who had been sent to Europe in 1882 to study constitutions of Western nations preparatory to drafting the Japanese constitution. . . .

In 1888 the Privy Council was created through the initiative of Ito, . . . who was its first president. Its function originally was to pass critical judgment on the Constitution, which was nearing completion. But after the promulgation of the Constitution in 1889, the Privy Council remained as the watchdog of autocratic rule. . . . [I]t was Ito's express opinion, . . . that the Constitution was a gift of the Emperor to his people not a concession to the demand of the people for a Constitution. Only the Emperor can initiate amendments to the Constitution which have to be approved by the Upper and Lower Houses, and its interpretation lies with the courts of the country and, in the last analysis, in the hands of the Privy Council. It was conceived in a spirit of benevolent autocracy and has remained as the inflexible instrument of absolutism.

Since any attempt to amend the Constitution by popular franchise, court decision or vote of either house separately or both together would put the initiator beyond the pale of legality, the greatest constitutional struggles in modern Japan have been fought over the question of suffrage, which was deliberately excluded by Ito from the Constitution and hence left open to legisla-tive change. For this reason many groups and parties sometimes not represented in the Diet, and more often parties associated with the Labor movement, have been active in the campaign to extend the franchise. . . .

The . . . course of Japanese liberalism was charted in the early eighties when its leaders, dismayed by the violent enthusiasm of their own followers and disheartened by government repression, retired to their tents and left the government in solitary command of the field. A few years later when Ito's handiwork was completed, the political leaders took their place in a Diet which had suffered emasculation in regard to such vital questions of government as control of the purse and power to amend the constitution. They had to participate in parliamentary government on terms which excluded all but negative power to block legislation or constitutional amendment initiated from above. Parliamentary leaders could at best be little more than spokesmen of public opinion or, to be more precise, spokesmen for some important section of the community. This role of tribune of the people has been honorably played by many Japanese parliamentarians, notably Ozaki Yukio, Abe Isoh, Inukai Tsuyoshi, . . . and other lesser figures. At worst, members became political careerists who by perfecting the art of obstruction could compel the government to silence them either by promotion or bribery.

Opposition to the Government has not been confined merely to politicians sitting in the Diet. Since the beginning of the 20th century opposition to the government of the most effective type, despite the severe Peace Preservation Act of 1900, came from labor and socialist parties, and in recent years from various military or fascist groups. The former have agitated for the radical extension of democracy through universal suffrage and improved labor legislation while the latter have urged the complete eradication of democracy on the ground that it favors corruption, inefficiency and national disunity.

The Fundamental Strength
of the Early Democratic Forces

NOBUTAKA IKE

Professor Ike, now a political scientist at Stanford University, followed in the scholastic footsteps of Dr. Norman, but he delved deeper into the political (as differentiated from the social and economic) aspects of what he calls the "democratic" movement (referred to by Norman as the "liberal" movement). He finds it more diversified in composition and more developed in ideology than did Norman; and thus more impregnated with democratic potential.

He also gives concrete examples of the impact of Western thought and local resistance to police oppression. Ike's study of the Meiji period, written after Japan's defeat in World War II, found much groundwork for democracy in recent Japanese history hidden behind the officially sponsored national ideology, which everyone was supposed to adhere to. This ideology consisted of feudalistic social myths — such as the divinity of the Emperor, the Confucian family system, and hierarchical social relationships — which were consciously remolded and enforced in the middle Meiji period, Ike argues, in order to restrict those contemporary democratic tendencies that greatly frightened the Meiji oligarchs. The crucial issue at the time was the amount of power the parliament would have. In Dr. Ike's opinion if the ideas of the democratic movement had been institutionalized, a radical shift in the leadership of modern Japan would have resulted.

T HE long-run significance of Itagaki's [first resignation from the Meiji government in 1873] was that it provided leadership for political opposition on a wide scale. In Itagaki the various individuals, groups, and interests at odds with the Meiji oligarchy found a leader of national stature. He had not only participated in the Restoration movement, but later had sat in the high council of state. He had been a member of the inner group that governed the country. Hence when he stepped down from the government and placed himself at the head of an opposition movement, he gave to it a kind of prestige and standing which no mere local political figure could have supplied.

Itagaki's assets as a leader, on the other hand, would have been worth little without a political organization which could lend him support. Lacking such support, he would probably have remained another politician without office. It is certainly to his credit that Itagaki was perceiving enough to see that if he were to challenge the government successfully he must organize a political following. . . .

[Itagaki fired his first shot against the Meiji oligarchy a few months after his resignation. His attack took the form of a

From Nobutaka Ike, *The Beginnings of Political Democracy in Japan* (Baltimore, 1950), pp. 60–62, 65, 67–71, 83, 85–86, 107–108, 110–112, 115, 117–121, 130, 132, 137, and 188–191. Reprinted by permission of the Johns Hopkins Press.

28   NOBUTAKA IKE

memorial calling for the establishment of an elective assembly.—ED.]

A few months after he submitted his memorial, Itagaki quit the capital and proceeded homeward to Tosa (modern Kochi prefecture). Years later in an essay giving his account of the origins of constitutional government in Japan, Itagaki wrote that in 1874 he had felt the need of forming a political party. It had been his opinion, moreover, that a "true" political party should be based on local units rather than on some central organization located in a big city.

Accordingly, shortly after his return to Tosa, Itagaki founded the *Risshisha* (Society for Fixing One's Aim in Life), the first important political society. . . .

According to a statement issued at the time of its formation, the society stood for self-government, local autonomy, natural rights, the establishment of a legislative assembly, and equality of all classes. "We, the thirty millions of people in Japan," it said, "are all equally endowed with certain definite rights, among which are those of enjoying and defending life and liberty, acquiring and possessing property, and obtaining a livelihood and pursuing happiness. These rights are by Nature bestowed upon all men, and, therefore, cannot be taken away by the power of any man." Thus Locke's philosophy was proclaimed in Japan almost a century after the American Declaration of Independence.

There was, however, another aspect of the *Risshisha* about which virtually nothing was known until the publication of some documents in 1939. These documents revealed that the *Risshisha* was a mutual-aid society for the economic rehabilitation of the *shizoku,* as the samurai were called after the Restoration. This helps to explain its name, which, it is believed, was taken from *Risshi-hen,* the title of the Japanese translation of Samuel Smiles' *Self-Help,* published in 1871 and read very widely.

The announcement circulated by the *Risshisha* is of considerable interest. "The Westerners," it began, "say that self-reliance is based on knowledge and that government rests on self-reliance." It noted that since the Restoration the peasants, artisans, and merchants "had not had time to push ahead by themselves and become an independent people. Moreover, the *shizoku* have not been able to maintain their former positions, and with the three classes are falling into servility and bigotry." Now only the *shizoku,* it was asserted, "possess some knowledge and have self-reliance." The document proposed, therefore, that the "four classes should freely associate as friends, help one another, and make up for each other's deficiencies." In other words, the *shizoku* would furnish knowledge and the spirit of self-reliance, while the plebeians would provide the capital and business experience. . . .

Although a few other political societies more or less patterned after the *Risshisha* were founded elsewhere, Itagaki's movement was still largely confined to Tosa. So in February, 1875, the leaders of the *Risshisha,* hoping to broaden the scope of operations, formed another society in Osaka called the *Aikokusha* (Society of Patriots). This society was intended to be the central headquarters for the democratic movement, but it collapsed very shortly. This was partly due to the lack of funds to maintain the organization; but an even more important cause was the opportunistic maneuvers of Itagaki, its moving spirit. . . .

In 1878 the leaders of the *Risshisha* revived the *Aikokusha* and began a concerted drive to organize local affiliates. Often they worked through influential local leaders. Speakers and organizers were also sent out by the *Aikokusha* to lend aid. As a technique of political agitation, it was discovered that public speeches were much more effective than the press, for by this method it was possible to reach even the illiterate peasant. Sometimes only one political speech was needed to form a small group consisting of several tens of members. Perhaps it was because of their effectiveness that the police were much concerned about such political speeches. The late Yoshino Sakuzo has told about an incident that occurred in Koriyama in Nara prefecture where the local police went to incredible lengths to prevent local leaders from holding a political rally. Day after day the police raised numerous and petty objections. But the sponsors, being equal to the challenge, met these objections with dogged persistence. The meetings, originally planned for October 6 to October 8, 1879, were finally scheduled to begin on the 12th. On the appointed day a crowd of more than 2,000 persons assembled at 10 o'clock in the morning. The police arrived and in a series of delaying tactics held up the rally until 3 o'clock in the afternoon. Then the police announced that the rally would not be allowed and ordered the crowd to disperse. Having waited for hours, the spectators were in no mood to obey. "We were born in isolated communities," they said, "and have neither books nor the ability to read them. We left our work and took the trouble to come, hoping to enrich our knowledge by coming into contact with scholars, and to obtain benefits equal to more than ten years of reading." The angry crowd then reassembled in front of the police station where they argued with the police officers. Finally when darkness fell they gave vent to their resentment by hurling stones and breaking the windows of the police station.

The efforts of Itagaki and his followers to expand the democratic movement produced astonishing results. The movement, hitherto largely confined to Tosa, now spread like a contagion. There was a remarkable proliferation of political societies. Exactly how many societies were formed in this period and how big a membership they boasted is not known. It is certain, however, that numerous groups were organized, particularly at the village level. It has been reported that in Tokyo-*fu* alone, there were twenty-two societies with a membership of more than 16,000 persons.

Some of the organizations in the larger towns and cities grew to be quite large. A well-known organization, the *Aikoku Ko-* *shinsha* (Patriotic Society) had more than 11,000 members. . . . [T]hese societies, like the Jacobin Clubs in revolutionary France and the Democratic-Republican societies in early America, included people from nearly all social strata, excluding only those at the very top of the social pyramid. Almost everyone was represented, for among the members one could find *shizoku*, wealthy landowners, rural industrialists, journalists, school teachers, peasants, tenant farmers, and laborers.

The leadership, however, was at first confined almost exclusively to the *shizoku* class. This was because the first spark that set off the democratic movement was samurai discontent. It has been noted that the memorial of 1874 had been a gesture of protest on the part of the "outs" against the "ins." Having initiated the movement, the samurai were able to maintain themselves in positions of leadership for several years. But after about 1878 they were obliged to give way more and more to the non-samurai. Several factors account for this shift. During these years economic attrition had taken a heavy toll among the *shizoku*. Reduced to penury, they could no longer afford to devote a large part of their time to politics. On the other hand, as the movement gained many adherents, the plebeians came to outnumber the *shizoku*. Since, moreover, they provided much of the funds, the non-samurai were bound to demand some say in the management of affairs. . . .

. . . For a concrete example of the shift in the leadership we may turn to the political convention held in Okayama in 1879. There an attempt was made to have *shizoku* appointed to the executive committee, but the opposition of the rank and file, consisting about eighty percent of plebeians, was so strong that it failed. Then the convention drew up a strong petition to the government saying that "When we seek the reason for the extension of popular rights in the history of the West, we see that the rulers did not grant popular rights, but rather that the people themselves took the initiative and seized them."

With the *shizoku* receding to the back-ground, the mantle fell on the shoulders of the rural aristocracy. True in some instances the *shizoku* remained in control, especially in the *Aikokusha* and its successors, and they still provided virtually all of the theorists and publicists. But in the majority of the local affiliates, which gave the democratic movement its momentum, the rural gentry were in command. . . .

By 1880 the rural aristocracy had captured the movement. In other words, the democratic movement was now being led by the same class that had joined the pro-Emperor cause against the Tokugawa a generation earlier. In fact there is at least one example where a big landowner in Fukui prefecture by the name of Sugita Senjuro was active in the anti-Tokugawa movement, and his son, Sadakazu, participated in the democratic movement. No doubt a careful search of local histories would reveal other instances of this kind, for it is generally known that political attitudes have a way of being transmitted from generation to generation. Some areas tend to be politically unstable, while in other areas the opposite is true. Probably it was no mere accident that areas like Nagano and Gumma, which were receptive to the pro-Emperor cause in the late Tokugawa era, actively supported the democratic movement some twenty years later.

*   *   *

. . . [T]he movement was initiated by a group of disaffected samurai who used democratic slogans to oppose the government in power. By the latter part of the 1870's, however, a number of political figures threw in their support. Rallying together landowners and tenant farmers, they organized political societies in the rural villages and towns. Almost always these local leaders were relatively wealthy landlords. In addition they were, in many instances, rural industrialists operating local breweries and small-scale industries producing goods on the domestic system.

As landowners and industrialists they op-posed the fiscal policies of the central government. They resented the fact that so much of the revenue was derived from the land tax. Moreover, they looked with misgivings on the steady flow of taxes into the central treasury, for this tended to drain the countryside of capital which otherwise could have gone into industrial development. . . .

Between 1878 and 1881 the democratic movement gained numerous adherents from the lower classes. Small landowners, tenant farmers, and wage workers swelled the ranks. Each group had reasons for enlisting in the new cause. The poorer peasants, like their wealthy neighbors, hoped for tax reductions. Seeing that the taxes they paid were not being used for their benefit but rather for the maintenance of the army, the police, the bureaucracy, for industrialization, and for debt charges on bonds held by the samurai, money lenders, and the nobility, they demanded "cheap government." The tenant farmer, weighted down by high rents, harassed by Nature, and perennially in debt, longed for some land that he could call his own. Caught in the squeeze between high prices and low wages, the wage worker wanted some kind of relief from his misery. All of them agreed that the system of compulsory military service was undesirable. Those on the farms found conscription particularly burdensome since it took away much needed labor. The incidence of service, moreover, was inequitable. By paying a sum of 270 *yen*, an amount, incidentally, which only the wealthy could afford to pay, one could escape being called. So strong was the opposition to conscription that it led to a number of peasant revolts. General Yamagata, the creator of the modern army, once complained that the people hated military service. "There are not a few," he said, "who injure themselves or run away, or by other fraudulent practices try to avoid being called."

The task of knitting together these diverse elements into a coherent movement was performed by some professional politicians like Itagaki and his friend, Goto

Shojiro. Although these men had their liberal moments, they were not above using the movement to further their personal careers. Gathered about them, however, were a number of writers and intellectuals. Genuinely moved by the heady doctrines of European and American democracy and sincerely desirous of seeing democracy planted in Japan, they rendered yeoman service. They advised the leaders and wrote many of their speeches for them. They peppered the government with stinging memorials, published long articles in newspapers extolling democratic rights, and even went on speaking tours in order to arouse their fellow citizens. In their speeches and writings they denounced the Meiji government for being a tight oligarchy of Sat-Cho politicians. In order to break the hold of this oligarchy and thus bring an end to the abuses, they said that a national assembly must be established. And so persuasively was this message conveyed and so ready were the people to receive it that by 1880 the cry for a national assembly swelled into a national chorus.

*   *   *

. . . [T]he *Jiyuto,* the most militant and radical of the major parties, drew its main strength from the rural areas. The *Kaishinto,* on the other hand, was more urban, but at the same time was frankly devoted to the interests of the wealthier classes. It can be said, therefore, that the urban groups which played a fairly important role in the rise of Western liberalism, were not represented in any significant degree in the Japanese democratic movement. Yet this should not be interpreted to mean that no attempt was made to enlist the support of the urban proletariat. In 1880 a number of intellectuals in Tosa spent a month or so pulling *jinrikisha.* By taking up this despised occupation they hoped to secure a following among the working classes, and to encourage the samurai to take up regular occupations. They published a manifesto in which they said that there was nothing

degrading about manual labor. They also wrote a series of articles in a Tosa newspaper describing their experiences. As a result of these articles, says one source, "the manual laborers at last became cognizant of their rights."

A more serious attempt to organize the rickshamen was made in Tokyo in 1882. At that time some radical members of the *Jiyuto* formed the *Shakaito* (Rickshamen's Party) and thereby tried to link up city workers with the *Jiyuto* movement. In the *Shakaito* then we have an interesting example of an urban movement which was in a sense an offshoot of the democratic movement stemming largely from the countryside. . . .

This alliance between the two groups proved to be short lived. Not long after the *Shakaito* was organized, . . . several [members] were arrested and imprisoned for fighting with the police. Thus the attempt to organize and enlist the aid of urban labor ended in failure.

*   *   *

Changing conditions called for new intellectual moorings. After the fall of the Shogunate, a freer atmosphere prevailed. The orthodox Confucian doctrines, which the Tokugawa rulers had fostered to facilitate their rule now seemed somewhat anachronistic. A redefinition of the relation of the individual to the state and to society was made necessary. And in the realm of political theory, as well as in more mundane matters like technology and military organization, the Japanese turned to their Western mentors for enlightenment and guidance.

The new generation of political theorists first turned to British Utilitarianism. For this they could hardly be blamed. The very fact that Utilitarianism was the dominant political philosophy of Britain, the great Power, must have been recommendation enough. Perhaps equally important was the fact that this doctrine, with its strong bias towards individualism, accorded well with the new temper in Japan. Furthermore, the simplicity of the formula, "the greatest happiness of the greatest number," which the Utilitarians used to explain social phenomena, no doubt appealed to the Japanese who by tradition were not interested in problems of profound philosophical nature. . . .

The first wave of Utilitarianism was quickly overtaken by successive waves of European thought. As the Japanese became more familiar with Western political thought, they became discriminating in their preferences. Increasingly different political groups began to choose the kind of political theory which best served their interest. The *Kaishinto,* for example, eventually became the repository of a somewhat modified form of the earlier Utilitarianism. The main body of the *Jiyuto* was attracted by Herbert Spencer. The radical wing of the *Jiyuto,* however, fell under the influence of French thought. Rousseau, whose *Social Contract* was first translated in 1877 became the guiding light of this group. Through their manifestoes, speeches and articles they popularized the doctrine of natural rights, and spread the idea of liberty and equality. . . .

Thus it can be said that English Utilitarianism and French political thought contributed to the strength of the democratic movement by providing it with an ideological basis. By turning to the writings of Mill, Spencer, and others the anti-government forces were able to secure ready-made arguments with which to embarrass the government. But, . . . not all Western thought was helpful. Prussian ideas of statecraft, by strengthening the position of the government, had the effect of weakening the democratic movement.

*   *   *

The transformation of Japan occurred at a time when socialism had already become a factor in European politics. Just four years before the Restoration, the First International was formed under the leadership of Marx. In 1871, while the Meiji government was still in the midst of re-organization, the Paris Commune fell. The growth of the democratic movement in Japan was roughly paralleled by the rise of the Social Democratic Party in Imperial Germany, and the emergence of Nihilism as an element in the politics of Tsarist Russia. Significantly enough the Japanese were in possession of some information, although not always accurate, concerning these European developments, and there is reason to believe that this knowledge affected the course of the democratic movement. . . .

Owing to the nature of the source of information, the Japanese public was never presented with a systematic treatment of the socialist doctrine. As a result many people apparently received the impression that socialism called for an egalitarian social order in which private property would be abolished. Thus the result was that not only conservatives but even liberals expressed strong opposition to socialism. One writer has examined the newspapers supporting the democratic movement in order to see how they reacted to the question of socialism. He found that they criticized the doctrine because, they said, it would lead to the end of private property. Many of the articles appearing in these newspapers staunchly defended private property, for to them it was the basis of security, livelihood, happiness, wealth, and progress. Modern democratic thought, it was claimed, rested on the system of private property. If property were abolished the social order would collapse and society would revert to a barbaric state. . . .

There was a general belief that socialist parties would be formed in Japan. "The spread of socialism," said the newspaper, *Azuma,* "will probably not stop on the continent of Europe . . . and it appears that it will spread to our empire. . . ." The press noted the existence of social and economic inequality in Japan and warned that if the government continued to suppress the democratic movement, the disaffected people would be forced to turn to socialism. Some of the papers contended that the way to prevent socialism in Japan was to establish constitutional government which would protect the rights and liberties of the people.

Actually, of course, there was no reason for the Japanese to be so apprehensive about socialism. Industrialization in Japan was still on a small scale, and as yet there existed no large and class-conscious proletariat. There was, on the other hand, ample grounds for the leaders of the movement to be extremely wary of any doctrine which would pave the way for the modification of existing property rights. It will be recalled that many of the leaders and wealthier members of the *Jiyuto* were landowners, renting out land to tenant farmers. Consequently, they were sensitive to pressure from landless peasants demanding cheaper rents and a more equitable distribution of land. In fact in the fall of 1882 there was formed an Oriental Socialist Party. . . . [T]his party was in reality a peasant party and socialist in name only. But to the rural propertied groups, who associated socialism with the abolition of private property, the formation of a peasant party which, from the name, appeared to adhere to socialistic principles, must have been a serious menace. . . .

*   *   *

[In turning for a moment to the intellectual origins of the democratic movement in Japan, one person we must mention is Ueki Emori.] His name flits in and out of Meiji history, for he was an active participant in politics, writing polemical articles, speaking to mass meetings, and organizing political societies. A list of books on liberal thought in the Meiji era would include at least eight titles by him. Nor would these account for all of his literary output. He was not only a frequent contributor to newspapers, but also drafted or wrote, it is suspected, many of Itagaki's speeches and articles. He was Itagaki's "brain trust" or as the Japanese historians put it, his "wisdom bag." . . .

Ueki envisaged a constitutional mon-

archy for Japan, with the state organized on a federal basis. His preference for such a scheme probably reflected to some extent the conflict between local interests and the growth of the central government. Involved also were patronage considerations, for local autonomy always provides more officers for local inhabitants.

According to Ueki's draft of a proposed constitution, the federal government was given certain powers. It could make laws governing relations between states; it could declare war and make peace, and conclude agreements with foreign countries. It had the exclusive power to levy customs duties and internal tariffs; it could control the postal service and make laws regulating the possession of arms. It could not, on the other hand, interfere in the internal affairs of the states, change boundaries without the permission of the states, or prevent new states from joining in the union.

The legislative power was to be vested in an unicameral legislature. . . .

. . . Ueki had a precocious understanding of the political process. He saw clearly what political reforms would be necessary if Japan were to become a democracy. He revealed his dislike for the autocratic Meiji government in no uncertain terms, writing and working against it when it was not always safe to do so. He probably made as spirited a defense of democratic government as has ever been made in Japan. Taking a considerable body of Western political thought, he clothed it partly in Japanese dress and made it available to his contemporaries. In so doing, he helped to provide the democratic movement with a critique of the existing order and a blueprint of the new. . . .

*   *   *

The history of Japanese politics in the twenty year period between the restoration and the promulgation of the constitution in 1889 was strongly influenced by the character of the Meiji Restoration. The balance of political forces at the end of the Tokugawa era and their peculiar alignment encouraged the subsequent growth of a strong centralized state. The conjunction of two crises in the middle of the nineteenth century: the internal economic crisis and the external pressure of the Western powers enabled an anti-Tokugawa faction led by a small group of low ranking but able samurai to effect a political revolution.

The symbols used in this movement, however, were traditionalist rather than revolutionary. The leaders of the Restoration gave their actions an aura of legitimacy by appealing to a remote past. The claim was put forward that the Shogun was an usurper and that the Emperor was merely being "restored" as the rightful head of the state. From the very beginning steps were taken to make the Emperor into an absolute monarch by reviving the ancient mythology which claimed for him divine origins. The Throne, it goes without saying, proved to be a useful tool for breaking down local loyalties and for creating a modern nation. Thus, in short, the scales were weighted in favor of the development of a regime in which power would be tightly held by a small group of men.

But, as has been shown in the foregoing pages, the group in power did not remain unchallenged. Some disaffected samurai, including a few who had been in the government, organized a popular movement to oppose those in control. From the point of view of the government this was a formidable movement because it had a more than rudimentary party organization and because one of the most important elements in it were the wealthier landowners and rural industrialists who had a firm grip on local government. Furthermore, one of the demands which the popular leaders made was the establishment of a national legislative assembly. The idea of an assembly had a fairly long history in Japan and it was difficult for the government to refuse these demands. In fact it was finally forced to call a Diet in 1890. The crucial issue, however, was the question of the amount of power which this assembly would have. If institutional arrangements which theo-

rists like Ueki Emori had advocated had been put into effect, the balance of political power in the state would have been radically altered. The center of power would have shifted from the small group of ex-samurai to the newly-created Diet consisting chiefly of men from the opposition parties. Since the most prominent of these parties was the *Jiyuto,* an important consequence of this might have been a marked change in the tempo of industrialization and modernization, for the landowner-rural industrialists who were influential in the *Jiyuto* would have hardly favored voting large appropriations for subsidizing modern urban industries and for building up a huge military establishment. Also if, as Ueki proposed, universal suffrage had been adopted, the way would have been opened for small landholders, tenant farmers, and industrial workers to have their interests represented in varying degrees in the government.

The fact is, however, that the democratic movement did not succeed in breaking the hold of the Meiji oligarchy; and it may be appropriate to present here some reflections as to why it ultimately failed. One of the most important reasons for its failure was the split within the *Jiyuto.* Such a split could have been avoided if the democratic movement had dealt adequately with the question of land reform. But this perhaps would have been asking for the impossible since the landowners who were powerful in the *Jiyuto* surely would have opposed such a move. A conclusion to be drawn from this is that the movement suffered from the lack of a more diversified basis of support. The fact that there existed no important groups of urban merchants and industrialists to join a movement of this kind resulted in serious weaknesses.

The second reason was inadequate leadership. Too often the leaders were willing to abandon the movement to take posts offered by the government. This may have been prompted in part by the persistence of class feeling which led the samurai to look upon themselves as forming a superior class best fitted for governing the nation.

Third, there was the matter of ideology. Although there were some theorists who had a precocious grasp of political theory, the movement was never able to produce an outstanding theorist of its own. In fact it could be said that the theorists for the democratic movement were men like John Stuart Mill, J. J. Rousseau, and Herbert Spencer. A practical consequence of this was the failure to produce new political symbols which could seriously compete with those available to the government, such as the Emperor. The advantage which the government enjoyed was that it could point to the Imperial court as an uniquely Japanese institution while those in the opposition could only appeal to universal concepts like natural rights. In a period of rising nationalism, this was an important factor.

This leads to the fourth reason, namely nationalism. Japan was modernized in a period when the Western powers were enlarging their colonial possessions by the use of military power. Like other Asiatic countries, Japan's sovereignty was impaired by the imposition of unequal treaties. The consequence of this was the growth of an exaggerated form of nationalism; and given their environment and history, the Japanese quickly learned the usefulness of armed might and began to emphasize military preparedness. Since the leaders of the democratic movement were themselves highly nationalistic, they were unwilling to oppose the principle of a strong state. They could only argue that an ingredient of national power was national unity and that the latter could be best obtained by providing wider representation for the various interests within the nation.

Finally, it is necessary to point to the remarkable ability of the Meiji leaders to grant concessions at the proper moment. Whenever popular pressure became too powerful to be suppressed, they would retreat without giving up the substance of power. They possessed the kind of suppleness which any regime wishing to remain in control must possess. Perhaps an explanation of this is to be found in the fact that these men were able to overthrow the Shogunate without having had to acquire a wide popular following. This left them unencumbered with commitments, thus enabling them to act freely as the occasion demanded.

*   *   *

In the foregoing analysis the factors favorable to the democratization of Japan have been purposely emphasized. The author does not wish to imply, however, that he believes that the emergence of a democratic Japan is a foregone conclusion. On the contrary, he is in sympathy with many of the books and articles that have appeared since the end of the war describing the numerous obstacles that exist. Occasionally, however, there is in these publications an assumption, implicit or explicit, that the Japanese are incapable of becoming democratic, for historical, cultural, or other reasons. With this assumption it is difficult to agree. The history of the democratic movement in the Meiji era shows conclusively that modernization was accompanied by the assertion that the masses of the people should have the right to bring the institutions of government under their control and thereby be able to run their own affairs. Not only did the democratic movement fail in the Meiji era; the realization that it might have succeeded provoked a reaction among the powerholders, who deliberately took steps to strengthen and elaborate the old social myths [such as the divinity of the Emperor, the Confucian family system, and hierarchical social relationships].

"TAISHŌ DEMOCRACY"
AND THE DECLINE OF "PARTY RULE"

On Applying Democracy in Japan —
An Optimistic Contemporary View (1916)

YOSHINO SAKUZŌ

The democratic spirit of the people's rights movement was rekindled in what was known as "Taisho democracy," a phenomenon much more complex and difficult to delimit chronologically. It was not coincident with the reign of the Taishō Emperor (1912–26) and did not become a popular expression until toward the end of the First World War, when Japan had joined the Allies and fought "to make the world safe for democracy." But an early phase of the movement can be traced to the first campaign "to protect constitutional government" of 1912–13.

The first important success of the movement was the elevation of Hara to the Premiership in 1918, for he was the first *bona-fide* party leader to hold that post. "Party rule" is often dated from that time, despite various subsequent setbacks. The spirit of "Taishō democracy" extended beyond 1926 to the assassination of Premier Inukai in 1932, marking the end of "party rule." Some authors, however, terminate the period of "Taishō democracy" earlier: in 1928 with the suppression of civil liberties under Premier Tanaka, or in 1927 with the outbreak of the financial panic. Periodization, however, is less important than an understanding of the easily deceptive terms, "Taishō democracy" and "party rule."

While some institutional changes were demanded, "Taishō democracy" was essentially a reinterpretation of the Meiji Constitution in such a way as to make popular government possible. A limitation on the House of Peers, an expansion of the role of the Diet, a strengthening of the powers of the Premier, and universal suffrage constituted some of the institutional demands. But they followed from what was called "the perfection of constitutional government," which, as we shall see, was an attempt to build a democratic groundwork behind the existing institutional façade.

The foremost theoretical exponent of this new democratic movement was Yoshino Sakuzō (1878–1933). The following selection, which appeared in 1916, probably did more than any of his other writings to establish this reputation. At that time he was an assistant professor on the Faculty of Law at Tōkyō Imperial University where he had received his training. He had already been an advisor to the Imperial Chinese government and spent the years 1910–13 studying and observing abroad, especially in Germany, England, and the United States. Subsequently he lent guidance to the democratic tendencies in

From Yoshino Sakuzō, "Mimponshugi ron," *Chūō Kōron* (January 1916), pp. 1–130, translated by Arthur Tiedemann in *Sources of the Japanese Tradition* (New York, 1958), pp. 725–746. Reprinted by permission of Columbia University Pr ess.

the student movement and threw himself into the campaign for universal suffrage. After a brief foray into politics — in which he helped organize the
Social Democratic (proletarian) Party in 1926 — he devoted himself to political and social criticism until his untimely death in 1933.

Rejecting the ideas of "popular sovereignty" and "natural rights" that
the thinkers of the people's rights movement had vaguely advocated, Yoshino
chose to build his theory of democracy on the "general welfare." For while
limitations on the imperial prerogative were antithetical to Japanese tradition
— even the Shōguns theoretically received their titles from the Emperor — the
Confucian tradition of "imperial benevolence" had long been accepted in
Japan, albeit in a peculiarly passive and Japanese form. The question was:
"How was the benevolent Emperor to know what was the general welfare?"
Here Yoshino borrowed central concepts from Utilitarianism, namely, that
the people can recognize individually their own welfare and the corollary of
this, that the welfare of the largest number of them constitutes the general
welfare. The people could best express themselves through a majority in the
Imperial Diet. Yoshino thus defined democracy functionally, as the best
mechanism for ascertaining the general welfare. The mechanism consisted not
only in having a parliament, but also in having a constitution that stands
above ordinary laws and defines and protects the democratic rights of freedom of speech, press, and assembly so that the people's will could be truly
expressed. Since the Meiji Constitution with its guarantees, despite loopholes,
existed, the road to democracy lay in its full realization and enforcement. A
further important implication was the extension of the suffrage, upon which no
constitutional limitations had been placed.

Yoshino synthesized elements from a number of sources. From Confucianism he took the concept of benevolent rule but attempted to set it upon a
democratic base by the use of Utilitarianism. From the English liberals he took
proposals for limiting powers of the old establishment (the Genrō and the bureaucracy, in the case of Japan) through enhancing the Diet, and for restricting
the influence of the new plutocracy through popular suffrage. He even borrowed slightly from the German organicists, who had influenced his former
teacher, Minobe Tatsukichi, for he accepted the analysis of the functioning
of the Meiji Constitution as in fact limiting the powers of the Emperor while
leaving the locus of sovereignty legally in the Emperor; but he did not go so
far as to accept the organic theory of the state. The foreign elements were
carefully used to reinterpret the traditional symbol of the Emperor. Thus, the
new democratic movement in prewar Japan set out by being at once more
modern and more Japanese than the earlier people's rights movement.

WHETHER or not constitutional government will work well is partly
a question of its structure and procedures,
but it is also very much a question of the
general level of the people's knowledge
and virtue. Only where the level is rather
mature can a constitutional government be
set up. . . . However, since the trend toward constitutional government is world
wide and can no longer be resisted, advanced thinkers must make the attempt
to establish it firmly. They should voluntarily assume the responsibility of instruct-
ing the people so as to train them in its
workings without delay. . . . This is not
a task which can be accomplished in a
day. Think of the situation in our own
country. We instituted constitutional government before the people were prepared
for it. As a result there have been many
failures, failures which have caused those
with high aspirations for government to
feel that we have accomplished very little.
Still, it is impossible to reverse course and
return to the old absolutism, so there is
nothing for us to do but cheerfully take
the road of reform and progress. Consequently, it is extremely important not to
rely upon politicians alone, but to make
use of the cooperative efforts of educators,

religious leaders, and thinkers in all areas of society. . . .

WHAT IS CONSTITUTIONAL GOVERNMENT?

The word "constitution" invariably means a nation's fundamental laws. However, when used as a modern political term it has certain additional connotations. . . .

First, one usually assigns to a constitution greater force than to ordinary laws. . . . Since a nation's fundamental laws are of great importance, the idea has persisted from antiquity that there should be a distinction between them and ordinary laws. However, there is another reason why modern nations give such special weight to constitutions. The intention is to prevent the reckless infringement, at some later time, of the rights which have been laid down in them with great care. Whatever they may ostensibly be, modern constitutions have in fact appeared as a result of the long struggle for popular rights which was waged against those who in the past monopolized political power — those rightly called the privileged classes. . . .

Second, a constitution must include as an important part of its contents the following three provisions: 1) guarantees of civil liberties; 2) the principle of the separation of the three branches of government; and 3) a popularly elected legislature. . . .

1. The fifteen articles comprising Chapter II of the Japanese Constitution concern "Rights and Duties of Subjects." As the title indicates, some of these articles prescribe duties, but most of them enumerate those rights and liberties which are indispensable to the people's material and spiritual happiness and progress. . . . It is clearly provided that these rights and liberties may not be arbitrarily restricted by the government, but can only be limited by law, in the enactment of which the Diet participates. . . .

2. If it is defined theoretically, the principle of separation of powers becomes a very troublesome problem. Generally speaking, it means that the executive, judicial, and legislative powers are exercised by separate organs of the government. . . . It is true for all countries without exception that the purport of the principle . . . is best shown in the area of judicial independence. However, nowadays its application to relations between the executive and legislative branches differs substantially from country to country. Of course, the executive and the legislature ought to be independent of each other, but if there is no provision at all for negotiations between the two, constitutional government cannot be expected to function smoothly. . . .

3. More than any other factor [provision for a popularly elected legislature] . . . is regarded by the public as the most important characteristic of a constitution. Indeed, there are many who think of it as the only essential characteristic of a constitution. . . . Why is this provision of such great importance? Because the popularly elected legislature is the only branch of government in the composition of which the people have a direct voice. The personnel of the other two branches are experts appointed by the government. The people have almost no direct concern in naming them. With the legislature it is just the opposite. Its members are directly elected by the people. Naturally, the people can exert influence upon it and thereby cause it to express fully the popular will. . . .

These are the [three] indispensable elements of a modern constitution. . . . If they are present, then there is a constitution. When such a constitution exists and is the guiding principle of political life, we have constitutional government. . . .

WHAT IS MEANT BY THE PERFECTION OF CONSTITUTIONAL GOVERNMENT?

Living as we do under a constitutional government we must work all the harder for its perfection. However we must not work blindly. The task requires a strenuous effort based upon the same . . . ideology that originally brought about the establishment of the Constitution and upon the fundamental spirit that lies concealed in its innermost depths. . . .

What then is the spirit of a constitution? No generalization is possible, for it varies from one country to another. . . . In some countries the privileged classes survive as relics of a bygone age and still continue to exercise their influence. Where this is so, even though the pressure of world trends has forced the promulgation of a constitution, there are many who try to implement it so as to do no injury to their antiquated political ideology. These people stridently emphasize the principle that their nation's constitution has nothing in common with that of any other, but instead possesses its own peculiar coloration. We frequently see the like in our country, where there is a tendency in constitutional theory to assert as the basis for the political structure a peculiar national morality of our own, attempting in this way to avoid interpreting the Constitution in accordance with Western constitutional ideas. . . . Of course, each country's constitution is tinged with that country's peculiar coloration. It would be difficult to summarize the unique qualities of each country's constitution, but it is possible to infer from the history of modern world civilization the spiritual basis common to them all. . . . The common spiritual basis which I discover in all constitutions is democracy.

THE SPIRITUAL BASIS OF CONSTITUTIONAL GOVERNMENT: DEMOCRACY

The Japanese word *mimpon shugi* (democracy) is of very recent use. Formerly *minshu shugi* seems to have been generally favored and even *minshū shugi* and *heimin shugi* have been used. However, *minshu shugi* is likely to be understood as referring to the theory held by the social democratic parties that "the sovereignty of the nation resides in the people." *Heimin shugi* implies an opposition between the common people (*heimin*) and the nobility, and there is the risk it will be misunderstood to mean that the nobility is the enemy and the common people are the friendly forces. By themselves the words *minshū shugi* are not liable to such a misinterpretation, but they smack of overemphasis on

the masses (*minshū*). Since . . . the basis of constitutional government is a universally accepted principle which politically emphasizes the people at large but which does not differentiate between nobles and commoners nor distinguish between a monarchical and a republican national polity, I suspect that the comparatively new term *mimpon shugi* is the most suitable. . . .

I think [the Western word] "democracy," as used in the fields of law and political science, has at least two distinct meanings. In one sense it means that "in law the sovereignty of the nation resides in the people." In the other it is used to mean that "in politics the fundamental end of the exercise of the nation's sovereignty should be the people." . . . I should like to use *minshu shugi* and *mimpon shugi*, respectively, as the suitable translations for these two senses of "democracy." . . .

In our country many people are prevented by the "popular sovereignty" aspect of *minshu shugi* from having a proper understanding of democracy. There has therefore been an unavoidable prejudice which has appreciably retarded democracy's development. Consequently, I believe that in order to have the people strive for the advancement of constitutional government with a correct understanding of democracy, it is extremely important to make clear the distinction between the two meanings of the word. . . .[1]

THE DISTINCTION BETWEEN POPULAR SOVEREIGNTY AND DEMOCRACY

Even "popular sovereignty," if we examine it closely, is seen to be of two kinds. . . .

[1] Hereafter *minshu shugi* will be rendered "popular sovereignty" to distinguish it from the term Yoshino prefers for "democracy"—*mimpon shugi.* Translator. [Actually, *mimpon shugi* was first used to denote a concept developed by Mencius, a Chinese Confucian in the 3rd century B.C. As a translation of "democracy," it received some acceptance in academic circles as a result of Yoshino's writing, but it never caught on as a popular term. Today *minshu shugi* is most widely used for "democracy" with all its connotations; the Japanese transliteration, *demokurashī*, however, comes a close second in popular usage and was in fact popular in Yoshino's day, too. Ed.]

The first has been set forth in the following form: In the corporate body known as the nation the original and natural locus of sovereignty must be the people as a whole. This I call absolute or philosophic popular sovereignty. . . .

The second kind is set forth in the following form: In a specific country it has been decided by interpretation of the constitution that the sovereignty resides in the people. This I call popular sovereignty by mutual consent or by interpretation. . . . Both types, however, concern the legal location of the nation's sovereignty. Consequently, there cannot be the slightest doubt that the word "popular sovereignty" is inappropriate to a country like ours, which from the beginning has been unmistakably monarchical. Therefore, I believe it is very clear that while "popular sovereignty" and "democracy" are verbally similar, they differ a great deal in substance, for "democracy" raises no question of republicanism or monarchism and constitutes the fundamental spirit common to the constitutions of all modern countries. . . .

MISINTERPRETATIONS OF DEMOCRACY

Democracy is not contingent upon where legal theory locates sovereignty. It merely implies that in the exercise of this sovereignty, the sovereign should always make it his policy to value the well-being and opinions of the people. . . . There is no doubt that even in a monarchy this principle can be honored without contravening the established system in the slightest degree. . . . Nevertheless there are many who think that democracy and the monarchical system are completely incompatible. This is a serious misconception. . . .

Most of the misconceptions about democracy arise from emotional arguments which have no theoretical basis. This is especially true of the small class that up to now has possessed special privileges and monopolized political power. . . . In the past the system made them rulers of the common people. In the new age they must yield this formal dominance to the people

and be content with the substance of moral leadership. . . . As long as they alter neither their attitudes nor their motives to accord with the change in the times, no true progress can be expected in constitutional government. The public is prone to say that constitutional government has failed to develop as we had hoped because the thought of the people has not developed. Yet, whether or not the people's thought develops is really determined by whether or not advanced thinkers properly guide it. When the small class of leaders holds to its narrow-minded views, it is impossible to implant in the hearts of the common people sound constitutional ideas no matter how much the necessity of spreading constitutional thought is preached. In this connection I must turn to the small enlightened intellectual class in the upper ranks of society and express the hope that they themselves achieve a true understanding of constitutional ideas and become conscious of their duty to guide the common people. . . .

In addition to misinterpretations based on emotional arguments, there are also criticisms of democracy which have a somewhat theoretical basis, or what would outwardly appear to be such. First, there are persons who confuse democracy with popular sovereignty and see no clear difference between them. They therefore think that democracy is opposed in theory to the principle of the sovereignty of the emperor. . . . Second, there are some who look at the history of democracy's development, see that it has invariably gone hand-in-hand with popular sovereignty, and conclude from this that it is incompatible with the monarchical system. . . . Up to a point, this theory is true. Indeed, if we look at the history of the development of constitutional governments, we see that they have for the most part passed through a revolutionary stage. . . . But it is a mistake to conclude that because in its origins constitutional government came from revolutionary democratic thought it must always be dangerous. This is as illogical as to argue that since man is descended from the monkeys he will always have the monkey's inferior characteristics. . . .

If we hesitate for fear of possible evil effects, progress and development will never be started. If something is necessary for the advancement of the nation and society, we must quickly search for a method to attain it. And we must strive greatly to prevent the abuses that we fear may result.

*   *   *

THE SUBSTANCE OF DEMOCRACY: POLITICAL OBJECTIVES

Earlier I defined democracy as the policy in exercising political power of valuing the profit, happiness, and opinions of the people. On the face of it, this definition reveals two aspects of democracy. First, the object of the exercise of political power . . . must be the people's welfare. Second, the policies which determine how political power is exercised . . . are settled in accordance with the people's opinions. . . .

The first requirement of democracy, then, is that the ultimate end of the exercise of political power be the good of the people. . . . In ancient times the objective of government was the survival and prosperity of a small number of powerful persons or the preservation of their authority; it was never the well-being of the people as a whole. . . . To the feudal mind, the land and people of a country were no more than the personal property of the royal family. But in the feudal period it became quite clear that land and people were the foundation upon which the royal family stood, so the people gradually came to be valued. . . . In general, international competition further deepened the ruling classes' feeling of dependence upon the people. . . . Accordingly, the feudal state came to treat the people with a great deal of consideration. . . . From our point of view today, the people were in the final analysis like servants happy under a kind-hearted master. They were not permitted to claim consideration for themselves as a matter of

right. . . . Our democracy is opposed to placing the people in such a position. It demands that the ultimate goal of government must change and become the welfare of the people. It further demands that . . . [their welfare] absolutely never be used as a means to some other end. In modern politics it is certainly not permissible to sacrifice the general welfare to the interests of a small number. . . .

There may still be some who denounce democracy as contravening the idea of loyalty to the emperor, a sentiment which dates from the founding of our country. . . . There may be those who ask whether democracy would oppose setting aside the people's welfare even if this were to be done in the interest of the Imperial Family. In my answer to these criticisms I would make the following two points. First, there is absolutely no contradiction nowadays between the "interest of the Imperial Family" and the interest of the nation, [an interest] which stands at the very top of the people's well-being. . . . Since the Imperial Family is the unique head of the national family, it is utterly unthinkable that it should become necessary "in the interest of the Imperial Family" to disregard the interest of the people. Consequently, I believe the interest of the Imperial Family and the interest of the people can never conflict with each other. Second, let us yield the point and suppose such a conflict to have arisen between the two. Since democracy relates to the sovereign's way of using his powers, there is nothing to prevent him from establishing the basic principle that he will not arbitrarily disregard the welfare of the people. . . . It is the determination of the Japanese people willingly to go through fire and water for the sake of the emperor. However, if the state systematically exploited this devotion to secure the people's acceptance of acts which disregarded the people's welfare, might not a certain cheerlessness come to characterize the subjects' spirit of loyalty? I would therefore like to make it a principle that whenever the State demands from the people sacrifices beyond a certain level the choice of whether or not they are to comply should be left entirely to their moral judgment. . . . Our loyal people will never for fear of their own safety hesitate to strive for emperor and country. Loyalty to the emperor is a spirit which dates from the founding of our country; it is the essence of our national polity. Reinforcing it by erecting it into a system would, I believe, lead to many evils but yield no advantage. . . .

Democracy does not permit the welfare of the people to be sacrificed for any purpose whatsoever. However, if we ask whether this point has today been completely realized in every country, [the answer is] most assuredly no. . . .

In our own country, unhappily, the people do not yet comprehend this problem and have not progressed to the point of insisting upon [the principle]. On the other hand, though in general the privileged classes have little by little come to understand the demands of the people and thus may be considered to be aware of the way in which to meet them, there are still narrow-minded persons in these classes who value themselves highly and are condescending to the people. . . .

In recent times there has been a trend in our country and others toward the appearance of certain new privileged classes in addition to the historic ones. Chief among these is the plutocracy. . . . It is contrary to the objective of democracy for economically superior and inferior classes to develop and as a consequence for profits to become the monopoly of a single class. Therefore, without touching on the fundamental problem of whether or not the organization of society should be basically reconstructed, it has of late been considered necessary in government to resort temporarily to moderate measures directed against these economically privileged classes. . . . To consider now the situation in our own country, in recent times capitalists have gained strength and with their huge financial power are finally on the point of wrongfully trampling upon the public in-

terest. It is true that this tendency is not so strong [in Japan] as it is in America and Europe, but recently the influence of the capitalists has increased markedly. After the Sino-Japanese War and the Russo-Japanese War their power grew with especial rapidity. Wealth has never lacked a certain degree of power, but before the Sino-Japanese War the money power was in fact completely under the control of political power. In the early years of the Meiji Period, wealth bent the knee at the door of political power and under the latter's shelter worked by degrees to increase financial power. . . . The Sino-Japanese War forced political power to beg aid from wealth for the first time. In this way wealth first achieved a position of equality with political power. With the Russo-Japanese War, the government of Prince Katsura kowtowed to the capitalists in all matters and sought their financial aid. Thereupon, wealth in one jump achieved strength sufficient to control political power. Bestowal of peerages on rich men dates from this time. . . . In this way the wealthy put pressure on political power and for the profit of their own class demanded the passage of various unfair laws. As a result there are in force today various kinds of financial legislation which are very disadvantageous to the general public and serve the interests of the capitalist class alone. Thus there has recently been produced in our country a new privileged class whose interests are unfairly protected by law. This kind of privileged class will in the future come into conflict with the demands of democracy; how the two will be harmonized is a matter which engages our most anxious attention. Since the moneyed class are concerned with things from a materialistic point of view, they do not readily listen to the voice of the ordinary people. Consequently, if there come to be great difficulties in solving problems in the area of [constitutional government], will they not in all likelihood arise from this problem of the financially privileged class? If the plutocracy were by some chance to make common cause with the traditional privileged classes in confronting democracy, there could be no greater misfortune for the nation. In this connection I must incessantly arouse the attention of the intellectuals and entreat the reflection of the nobility and the plutocrats who are flouting the affections of the nation. . . .

THE SUBSTANCE OF DEMOCRACY:
DETERMINATION OF POLICIES

Democracy not only implies that the end of government is the welfare of the people, but also demands that in the final determination of policies the people's opinions must be valued highly. This certainly does not mean that in each individual problem the opinions of each individual person be heard. It is an overall principle according to which nothing is done in opposition to the views of the people and no political action is undertaken without their general approval — expressed or tacit. . . .

However, one encounters quite strong criticisms of this second essential of democracy. If one examines these criticisms closely, they are, I think, seen to be of three kinds.

The first is the idea that democracy is opposed constitutionally to the principle of imperial sovereignty. . . . Yet, democracy is a theory of politics, not of law. From the legal standpoint, sovereignty resides in the emperor. Democracy comes in when one asks what principle ought to guide the emperor in the exercise of his sovereignty. It is in no way inconsistent with monarchy. Of course, I too am agreed that in order to protect the imperial institution we should reject the dangerous theory of popular sovereignty. However, opposition on this account to the advance of democracy — so similar in name to popular sovereignty, but so different from it in substance — is a serious problem for the future of constitutional government. . . .

Another criticism is the notion that, even conceding democracy to be a political concept, if in the exercise of his power the sovereign must by custom always take into account the general will of the people, his sovereignty is thereby limited and free exercise of his authority is prevented. However, those who believe this ignore the fact that in a constitutional country the sovereignty of the ruler is always limited in some way. It is because the word "limitation" is used that the above impression is produced; how would it be if the word "Way" were used in its place? Assume that constitutional government is a system under which a sovereign rules not by arbitrary whim but in accordance with the "Way." Is not this "Way" a sort of limitation on the free exercise of sovereignty? Well, the "Way" manifests itself both legally and politically; in other words, constitutional countries make it a rule to limit the power of the sovereign both in legal theory and in political practice. . . . Practically speaking, there is no country in the world today in which the sovereign decides all the policies of state by himself. . . . [Thus] the real problem is: what *kind* of limitations should there be on the ruler's authority? Should he be limited by concern for the will of the people generally, or by the opinions of two or three of his intimates? Concern for the will of the people may or may not be a limitation of the ruler's sovereignty, but I find it a one-sided argument not to admit that other limitations exist even when there is no such concern. Let us assume, for example, that there has been a cabinet change, and that custom demands that responsibility for forming a successor cabinet must be left to the leader of the political party that commands a majority in the parliament. It is objected that this practice imposes limitations on the ruler's sovereignty. . . . The ruler's complete freedom of action, if applied literally on such an occasion, would imply that without consulting anyone else he alone must decide who was to be the prime minister. . . . Yet, whether or not such a method would be practical, in fact the usual practice is for him to consult with two or three of the experienced ministers of his court. . . . As I see it, appointment of ministers according to party majorities in parliament and appointment on the advice of elder statesmen are both alike limitations of the ruler's authority. . . . The question which arises here is *which* sort of limitation should the ruler accept? Should he consult a small number of people, or should he consult at large with great numbers of people? Consequently, it is improper to reject democracy on the grounds that it limits the emperor's sovereignty and is therefore bad. If one wishes validly to reject democracy, one must go a step further and clearly demonstrate that it is always bad to take counsel with many men and always good to take counsel with a few men. Yet, in Japan since early Meiji it has been the fundamental national policy to take counsel with large numbers of persons. H. M., the Meiji Emperor, decreed at the beginning of the Restoration that deliberative assemblies should be widely established and all matters decided by public discussion. Thus the spirit of democracy, which consists in the just and equitable conduct of government in consultation with the majority of the people, has been our national policy since early in Meiji. Those who today deny this and advocate the principle of minority advice are moving counter to the general trend of political evolution. . . .

It is said that the enlightened are always likely to be a minority; that therefore the best government must be government by the minority; and that majority rule, on the other hand, deteriorates into mob rule. This . . . is partly true. However, one must not forget that minority rule is always government in a dark chamber. However splendid a person's character may be, when others do not observe him he is likely to commit excesses. . . . Some point to the corruption of the Diet and its members and say that there are bound to be evils in majority rule. . . . Yet in general, since government by the minority is secret government, many of its evils never come to the attention of the country; while since majority government is open government, there is a tendency to magnify its minutest deficiencies. . . .

It may be mistakenly thought that in majority government no use at all is made of the enlightened minority, but this is absolutely not so. . . . [This minority] can most properly fulfill their function as truly enlightened people when they modestly identify themselves with the majority, ostensibly following the majority will and yet as the spiritual leaders of the majority quietly working for the public good. . . . In all formal respects, the majority form the basis for the exercise of governmental power and they must be the political rulers, but within their ranks they in fact have need of spiritual leaders. . . . If the enlightened minority are truly to serve the national society, they must resolve to use their wisdom to guide the masses spiritually. At the same time they must resolve to enlist themselves in the service of the masses and by making their own influence prevail work for the public good. . . . Only when these two groups work in cooperation can there be a perfect development of constitutional government. Seen politically, this cooperation means the country is ruled by the will of the majority, but seen spiritually, it means the country is guided by the enlightened minority. . . . It is government by the people, but in one sense it can also be called government by the best. Thus one can claim that constitutional government reaches its most splendid perfection when there is a harmonious reconciliation of political democracy with spiritual aristocracy. . . . In this respect, I am thoroughly disgusted with the attitude of Japan's elder statesmen and other bureaucratic statesmen. Though they enjoy the special favor of the Imperial House and the esteem of the nation, they sometimes use their exalted position to interfere irresponsibly in political affairs. They will not reach down from their eminent position to establish contact with the masses, but instead take a hostile attitude toward democratic influences. It is much to be regretted that they thus fail to understand the true meaning of modern political life, but one must say it is especially unfortunate for the nation that they neglect the social function of the enlightened minority by not assuming the responsibility of popular leadership. After all, the ordinary people, surprisingly enough, actually pay an excessive respect to honors and titles. When the aristocrats who inherit historical and social authority are at the same time highly capable in point of actual ability and will jointly undertake the leadership of the people, the people gladly submit to this leadership. For the sake of the healthy development of constitutional government, nay, say rather for the sake of the future success of our society and nation, I entreat the enlightened minority to reflect deeply on this. We must hope that the aristocrats and pluocrats will respond to the handsome treatment they have received from the nation not only by giving great thought to how they should conduct themselves but also by giving serious attention to the education of their children and younger brothers. . . .

THE RELATION OF THE PEOPLE
TO THE LEGISLATORS

The most important point regarding the relation between the people and the legislators is that the people always occupy the position of master of the house, while the legislators are of necessity transients. The proper maintenance of this relationship is absolutely essential to the functioning of constitutional government. The abuses of constitutional government generally stem from the inversion of this relationship. And it is not just a question of the relation between the people and the legislators. The same truth holds as between legislators and the government. Whenever the legislators, who should supervise the government, are puppets of the government, many evils arise. Likewise, whenever the people, who should supervise the legislators, are instead manipulated by the latter, then the operation of constitutional government is replete with innumerable scandalous corruptions. If the government seduces legislators with offers of gain, if legislators also lead the people astray with offers of gain, then the proper relationships are inverted and

the structure of constitutional government is filled with abuses. If we wish to clean up political life and see a normal evolution of constitutional government, the first thing we must do is to pay strict attention to rectifying the relationship between the people and the legislators. There are at least three measures that must be adopted in order to accomplish this. . . .

1. Inculcation of election ethics. . . . I do not think that the ethics of the Japanese are, broadly speaking, especially low. Yet, since elections are a new experience for them, they have, regrettably, greatly ignored morality in conducting them. I feel it is necessary for us to inculcate the principles of election ethics in the people of the nation.

This being the case, what points should the people be made especially to understand? One of them is that though a single vote seems to be of very little importance, it actually is of great consequence to the fate of the nation. It is too sacred to be subject to influence by bribes or intimidation. A second point is that one votes in the interest of the nation, not for the profit of a single locality. To vote with local interests alone in view is likely more often than not to result in sacrificing the interests of the whole nation. A third point is that voting is our prerogative, not something to be done at the solicitation of the candidates. It is up to us to recommend proper candidates to the nation. Nowadays it is extremely important to drive these three points into the minds of the people. . . .

2. The necessity of adopting and enforcing strict election regulations. When legislators manipulate the people, invariably corruption and bad government flourish. Only when the people control their legislators does the operation of constitutional government follow the proper course. Therefore, it is especially important to impose strict penalties on the corrupt practices which may be carried on between the legislators and the people. . . . In this respect, a rather strict election law has been adopted in Japan; the only thing to be regretted is that it has not been rigorously enough en-

forced, and that the government tends to be lax in dealing with the activities of its own party. . . .

3. The necessity of extending the suffrage as widely as possible. If the suffrage is limited, corrupt practices are carried on unreservedly. When the suffrage is extended to the limit, there can be absolutely no distribution of bribes and the like. Moreover, only when it has become absolutely impossible for candidates to fight one another with money and things of value will they compete by sincerely and frankly presenting their views and personal qualifications to the people. Consequently, the people will gain an opportunity of receiving a political education through this means. When suffrage is limited, as it is today, there is a chance of winning a contest without presenting one's views and qualifications. Therefore the political parties pay little heed to the political education of the people. . . . There is no doubt that politically Diet members truly represent all the people of the country. Therefore, they should not be only the representatives of one class. It is logical then that the scope of the electorate should be as broad as possible. . . . Whether or not women should be excluded is, in the final analysis, a problem for the future. Today, suffrage is generally the exclusive possession of men. Of course there are some countries that do extend political rights to women. . . .

Nowadays the two ways that have actually been adopted to weed out those unsuited [to exercise voting rights] are educational qualifications and property qualifications. . . . However, these days formal education alone is not the thing which distinguishes between those who have and those who have not the training proper to humanistic [moral] cultivation. In a time like today when formal education is extremely widespread, I suspect that this standard is of little practical value. Making educational requirements an absolute qualification is behind the times. . . . Furthermore . . . limitation [on the basis of taxation or property] has become meaningless

in the present age. Practically, it is impossible to use a fixed amount of property as a criterion for mechanically distinguishing between those who have and those who do not have steadiness of character. . . .

Most of the civilized countries of the world have seen fit to adopt universal [manhood] suffrage. The only civilized countries . . . that impose comparatively great limitations on suffrage are Russia and Japan. In all other civilized countries universal suffrage is already a settled issue and no longer comes up for political discussion. In Japan the agitation for extending the suffrage has recently increased, but it will apparently take a long time before the idea becomes generally accepted. . . . Among many Japanese intellectuals there is an incredible misunderstanding of and violent antipathy to universal suffrage. Of course, in the beginning it was mainly the Socialists who advocated the system. This is by and large the probable reason for the misunderstanding. It is not strange that the upper classes are not pleased with the system, but it is a very peculiar phenomenon that the ordinary people do not welcome it wholeheartedly. A bill for the adoption of universal suffrage passed the House of Representatives at the 27th Diet in 1911, but at the time it was said that it was passed in the firm belief that it would never be approved by the House of Peers. As had been expected, the House of Peers rejected it by a huge majority. If we do not dispel this misunderstanding of universal suffrage and instill in the people the deep, heartfelt conviction that constitutional government cannot possibly develop properly unless universal suffrage is adopted, then the prospects for constitutional government are indeed gloomy. As a consequence of our present suffrage limitations, no more than three per cent of all Japanese are enfranchised. In the general elections of March last year [1915] only 1,544,725 persons had the right to vote. . . .

Thus, the extension of the suffrage and the strict enforcement of electoral laws are the most pressing matters facing Japan. The history of other countries shows that these two actions have often effected a cleanup in political life. . . .

THE RELATION OF PARLIAMENT TO THE GOVERNMENT

It is the government that takes direct charge of state affairs. Only when parliament oversees the government can there be just and equitable administration. But since the government wields real power, it is likely to use its position to control and manipulate the legislators, thereby reversing matters and ordering about as it pleases the very persons by whom, properly speaking, it should be supervised. Many hidden evils spring from such a situation. . . . Therefore, it is quite essential to the healthy functioning of constitutional government that the government be kept in a state of strict subordination to the parliament. . . .

Hence we consider it essential to sharpen the moral conscience of officeholders as much as possible. . . . Fidelity to conscience and regard for integrity are the very life and soul of a politician. For a politician there is no greater crime than to change his opinion for the sake of dishonest gain. It is strange that such affairs should be problems in a constitutional country. It is more than strange; it is shameful. Under constitutional government, worthless individuals should not become legislators in the first place. Government is fundamentally a very exalted calling, one that can only be undertaken well by persons of high cultivation. . . . The frequent occurrence of corrupt behavior among legislators is probably a peculiarity of Japan. With such a state of affairs it is absolutely impossible for constitutional government to progress in Japan. To prevent [corruption], as I have said again and again, it is necessary to keep the people from committing errors at the very start in the elections. Moreover, it is extremely necessary that the people inflict the severest punishments upon representatives who defile their of-

fices. We must not only by means of law sternly punish any representatives who defile their offices; we must also resolve to employ the power of public opinion to bury them in political oblivion.

In this regard, one point I wish to emphasize most sharply is that the offense of one who tempts [an official] is far more serious than that of the one who is tempted. . . .

Making the legislators morally independent of the government is only the first step. If we are to get the legislators fully to discharge their supervisory responsibility and thoroughly inquire into transgressions of the government, it is also essential that the government be made to fulfill its political responsibility to the parliament. . . . If the principle of responsible cabinets has not been firmly established in political institutions or usage, it is impossible to achieve the proper relationship between the government and the parliament. Consequently the requisites for democracy cannot be fully met.

In contrast to the responsible cabinet system there is also the principle of the nonparty cabinet. According to this idea, the cabinet should rise above the wishes of parliament and occupy a position of absolute independence. Under this system, no matter how much the government is opposed by parliament, no matter even if on occasion there are votes of nonconfidence [in parliament], the government unconcernedly continues in office. To put the theory in its worst light, it is a pretext which enables the government freely to perpetrate any kind of arbitrary misrule. Thus it is inconsistent with the principle that final decisions on policy should depend upon the views of the people generally. Therefore, the nonparty cabinet system is decidedly not the normal rule in constitutional government. Of course, under our Constitution theoretically the ministers of state are responsible to the sovereign alone, so it is not absolutely necessary for them immediately and as a matter of course to resign their posts when the Diet opposes them. That is to say, it cannot be called unconstitutional. However, it is clear from the foregoing that it is contrary to the spirit of constitutional government. . . .

The usual method used nowadays for calling the responsibility [of the government] into account is the parliamentary cabinet system. In most countries it has recently become the practice for the government to be formed by the leader of the political party that has a majority in parliament. In this sense most governments are today party cabinets. . . . In countries where there are just two major parties, this system works well, but in those with many small parties, it does not. . . . In order that the wisdom of the party cabinet system may be demonstrated, it is absolutely necessary to encourage the establishment of two major parties. However, the coming into being of two major parties is a matter which is determined by the course of events, and cannot very well be controlled by a constitution's theory. As a result, the workability of the party cabinet system always varies from one country to another. Hence the problem arises as to whether party government can really work smoothly in Japan. . . . Since I am interested in the progress of constitutional government in Japan, I should like to present to the nation the reasons why the natural trend toward a two-party system should be promoted and why the factors that stand in its way should be removed with the utmost vigor. Unfortunately there are a number of politicians who are in the grip of petty feelings and deliberately build up differences. These men are too narrow-minded to discard petty differences and form a union based upon greater common interests. They are sulky political malcontents who hide behind beautiful phrases such as "remaining loyal through ten years of adversity." The great misfortune of Japan today is the narrow-mindedness of politicians. . . .

I have explained why a fully responsible cabinet system must be adopted if constitutional government is to reach its most perfect development. However, in the West this matter was settled long ago and is hardly an issue any more. . . .

As I see it, Japan is, in general, on the right track in this respect. Though the responsible cabinet system has not been fully attained, today everyone seems to hold the firm belief that a vote of nonconfidence in the Diet should inevitably result in the resignation of the cabinet. Consequently it has become the practice for the government always to dissolve the Diet as soon as it sees that a nonconfidence motion is definitely about to be passed. Since December, 1885, when Count Itō . . . first instituted the present cabinet system, there have been about twenty cabinet changes. The great majority of them resulted from clashes with the Diet. Even in the beginning when the principle of nonparty cabinets was asserted, no cabinet could maintain its position in the face of parliamentary opposition. . . . At that time a nonparty cabinet seems to have meant a cabinet which stood aloof from the political parties in the Diet; it does not seem to have meant a cabinet uninfluenced by Diet decisions. Half-way through this thirty year period, Katsura and Saionji inaugurated the custom of alternating with each other as prime minister. Since that time, though the principle of party cabinets has not yet been fully implemented, it has become impossible for anyone to enter the cabinet without allying himself in some fashion or other with the majority forces in the Diet. We should endeavor to promote this tendency and attain a more thorough enforcement of party government. From this point of view, I believe that even though good results might temporarily be achieved with a national unity cabinet, such as has been advocated from time to time, or with the cabinet of "talents" that some schemers have occasionally dreamed of, we must firmly reject these for the sake of the progress of constitutional government. . . .

It is essential to the operation of constitutional government that parliament should be the central force in government. This is why we have preached the principle of responsible cabinets. Yet, the West has gone ahead to a still further stage of development. Namely, in one or two countries it is no longer the government that is the powerful obstruction to making parliament, especially the popularly elected house, the central political force. If there is anything today that still somewhat stands in the way of the political supremacy of the popularly elected house, it is the upper house. Hence it has come to be advocated that the lower house should be made supreme over the upper house. . . . Originally the upper house [was established as a body whose] duty it was to give further consideration to the decisions of the lower house because it was felt that the people, whom the lower house represents, were not yet sufficiently well informed. . . .

The advanced nations of the West believe the popularly elected house is extremely important to the functioning of constitutional government. They believe this because the essence of constitutional government is, after all, democracy; and the complete realization of democracy, presupposing as it does the various reforms I have mentioned above, ultimately consists in making the lower house the central political force. . . . In Japan the meeting of a responsible cabinet is only now becoming clear. Though this is cause for rejoicing, we must at the same time regret very much that the authority of the lower house, which directly represents the power of the people, is not very important. This is partly because the legislators that comprise it are not as yet endowed with knowledge and dignity. No matter how important the lower house ought to be in the governmental system, the authority of the nation will never be vested in it if those who actually make up its membership consist solely of mediocre, unprincipled fools. Because able men are not attracted into it, it lacks the authority to deal with the upper house; and when a cabinet is formed the unseemly truth is that at the very least the prime minister must be sought outside of the lower house. As long as the lower house lacks able men, it will lack power; as long as it lacks power, men of promise will seek careers elsewhere. In this vicious circle the wisdom of the responsible cabinet system cannot be fully demonstrated. Under the present circumstances it is useless for the lower house to assume an air of importance. Screaming that the lower house should be respected will not endow it with any actual power. In this matter, we must on the one hand earnestly seek self-respect and strenuous effort from the legislators; on the other, we must ardently hope that the people will not go astray in elections, and that they will not neglect to spur on, indirectly and directly, the legislators whom they have chosen. As regards the Elder Statesmen and other upper class politicians, we must earnestly hope that they do not assume an attitude of detached loftiness, of useless disparagement of the lower house and of disdain for the power of the people's representatives. We must earnestly hope that as Japanese they too will, like us, cooperate for the sake of the nation in the task of strengthening the lower house.

On the Obstacles to Democracy in Japan —
A Pessimistic Contemporary View (1918)

OZAKI YUKIO

Ozaki Yukio (1858–1954) became increasingly bitter concerning the prospects of democracy in Japan. He even disassociated himself from the over-enthusiasm engendered by the democratization efforts of the Allied Occupation after World War II. While he shared aspirations for democratic government with Yoshino and agreed with him in centering sovereignty in the Emperor, he was a practicing politician already halfway through his career at the time of the inception of "party government" when he wrote the following selection.

Ozaki's was a remarkable career. He resigned from the government in 1881 in sympathy with Ōkuma's forced resignation and then helped him form the Kaishintō (which he calls the Progressionist Party) the following year. After a trip abroad, he was elected to the first session of the Imperial Diet in 1890 and was reelected to the Diet in every one of the twenty-four subsequent elections until 1952.

In 1898, Ozaki became Education Minister in the coalition cabinet of Ōkuma and Itagaki. During that time, he made his famous speech attacking the plutocracy in which he used the phrase, "just suppose that Japan were a republic," to make a point. He was immediately attacked by anti-party newspapers and then deserted by Itagaki and even Ōkuma. The astonished Ozaki at first refused to resign; he considered the parties to have abandoned principle in not defending his really innocuous utterance. This was perhaps not the very beginning of his disillusionment but thereafter he put principle above loyalty to a party leader. He shifted allegiance considerably, most often remaining independent, the almost lone "voice of Japanese democracy," as he considered himself. Although he did become Minister of Justice in the Ōkuma Cabinet (1914–16), he never took another cabinet post but utilized his considerable talents as mayor of Tōkyō.

While Ozaki emphasized cabinet responsibility, he caustically criticized Japanese political parties for their strong *oyabun-kobun* (master-servant) ties, and for their alacrity in using governmental powers, such as those of the Home Ministry, for their own electoral advantage. He often despaired of the Japanese Diet ever attaining the effectiveness of the British Parliament which he admired.

Among the other obstacles facing Japanese politicians Ozaki singles out in the following selection the special prerogatives of the military and the civil bureaucracy. Actually, the politicians made certain gains under Premier Hara, who took office the very year Ozaki wrote the essay.

From Ozaki Yukio, *The Voice of Japanese Democracy: Being an Essay on Constitutional Loyalty*, translated by J. D. de Becker (Yokohama, 1918), pp. 19–22, 59–68, 75–82, and 89–97.

OUR NATIONAL CONSTITUTION AND
THE PARTY CABINET

There are persons who consider that the party cabinet is contrary to our national constitution and detrimental to the authority of the Imperial House; but let us briefly examine whether the opinion is well-founded.

"Party cabinet," "responsible cabinet," "parliamentary government," "party government" — these various expressions really refer to the same thing, or nearly the same thing — that is, to a system under which government is carried on in accordance with the wishes of the majority of the people. If it be once granted that the harmonious agreement of the will of the sovereign with the sentiments of the people is the essence and flower of our national constitution, and the fundamental cause of the esteem in which the Imperial House is held, what reason can there be for objecting to a system having such an aim? The party cabinet system is the best plan for securing the agreement of the will of the sovereign with the sentiments of the people. *"The welfare of the whole nation shall be promoted by the everlasting efforts of both the governing and governed classes,"* reads the second article of the Emperor Meiji's coronation oath. If it is desirable that ruler and ruled should act in concert, it is absolutely essential that the sentiments of the people, or public opinion, should be ascertained in order that the same may be either guided or acted upon. In order to effect this, no better means can be devised than that parliamentary members elected by the people should participate in the government; and it was doubtless this consideration that induced the Emperor to proclaim, in the first article of the said oath, that *"a Public assembly shall be established, and affairs of state shall be decided in accordance with public opinion."*

When the decision of all the affairs of state in accordance with public opinion has once been adopted as a principle of government, the budget and laws must be based upon that principle. If there is good reason to believe that the House of Representatives really does not represent the views of the majority of the nation, then it should be dissolved so that it may be filled by new members who correctly represent such views.

The next question to be considered in this connection is in what manner the heads of the administration, who are responsible for the enforcement of the budget and laws, ought to be chosen. When His Majesty the Emperor appoints the Prime Minister and other heads of the administration, should he choose them (1) from among influential statesmen popular with the bulk of the people, or (2) at his sole pleasure and discretion without any reference to public opinion? For even the same budget and laws may differ largely in effect according to the personality of the men who are charged with their enforcement. The people therefore naturally desire that the budget and laws should not merely conform with their views, but that they should be enforced by the heads of an administration chosen from among those statesmen who enjoy general confidence. That this is but a natural and reasonable desire admits of no doubt whatsoever. But I will now proceed to consider the matter, not from the view-point of the people, but mainly from that of the sovereign.

Which of the two methods of appointment above referred to is best calculated to attain the great object of "deciding all the affairs of state in accordance with public opinion" and of "the governing and governed classes acting in concert and actively carrying out social and political measures"? Which is the most convenient in principle for the purpose of securing a complete understanding between the sovereign and people? Which is the most effective means of fostering and strengthening the popular regard and reverence for the Imperial House? Having these objects in view, the better and more advantageous of the two methods of appointing cabinet ministers is so obvious that argument on the subject is almost superfluous. . . .

In view of events since the inauguration of the *Regulations Concerning the Organization of the Cabinet* in 1885 to the present day, it would appear that the following have become fixed and unchangeable precedents, namely:—

(1) When the Emperor desires a new cabinet to be formed, he first summons the statesman whom he intends to be the new Minister President [or Prime Minister or Premier] and orders him to form a cabinet;

(2) The statesman who has received the order then withdraws from the Imperial presence, and after selecting his colleagues in the new Cabinet submits them to the Emperor;

(3) The Emperor invariably approves of this recommendation, and appoints all the cabinet ministers in accordance with the desire of the statesman who has been ordered to organize the cabinet;

(4) When the Minister President retires from office, all the other ministers of state tender their resignations at the same time;

(5) In the event of a vacancy occurring in the cabinet subsequent to its formation, such vacancy is always filled by the Emperor, likewise acting on the suggestion of the Minister President.

If my memory does not mislead me, these five items were invariably observed by His Majesty the late [Meiji] Emperor ever since the Cabinet system was established — an example which has been followed by His Majesty the present [Taishō] Emperor. Confirmed as they are by the usage of two reigns, they may be regarded as fixed and immutable precedents upon which the following principles are based, namely:—

(a) Our Ministers of State are not singly and severally appointed, but jointly and collectively and upon the recommendation of the (prospective) Minister President;

(b) When they retire from office they also do so conjointly with the Minister President, except under special circumstances.

Whether the cabinet is (*a*) an integral body with the Minister President for its centre or (*b*) an assembly formed of several ministers of state acting each upon his own responsibility, has long been a moot question in Europe. In England, it has been decided, only after disputes extending over many years, that the ministers of state form a body which must stand and fall conjointly. Joint responsibility being the outcome of this decision, it therefore forms the backbone of party government.

If ministers of state were independent of each other and the cabinet simply their meeting place, the Sovereign might appoint and dismiss them individually without awaiting the recommendation of the Minister President; the ministers of state would remain in and go out of office separately instead of jointly and they would act, as a rule, each upon his own responsibility and only in exceptional cases upon their joint responsibility.

Owing to differences in national organization, things have happened in Europe which could hardly be dreamt of by the people of this country. I refer to the fact that in some countries conflicts for power between the Sovereign and the parliament or disputes with his cabinet ministers have occasionally happened. In such cases — more especially the latter — it is convenient for the Sovereign to be invested with power to appoint and dismiss his ministers separately, so that he may prevent their union and cause them to divert and control each other. This is why in former times a majority of the sovereigns of European countries persisted in upholding the principle of individual appointment and dismissal; some do so even to this day, but only in countries where the relations between sovereign and subject are not so clearly defined as in Japan.

If we examine the Imperial Constitution in regard to the Emperor's power to appoint and dismiss ministers of state, it of course admits of no doubt whatsoever that he has power to appoint and dismiss cabinet ministers separately and without awaiting the recommendation of the Minister President. But the position of our Imperial House is such, and the relations between sovereign and subject are so clearly defined, that there is neither reason why, nor circumstances under which, it may be desirable that they should be separately appointed and dismissed. Hence the great Emperor Meiji, from the time the cabinet system was first organized, graciously ordained that the cabinet should be an integral body, and adopted the system of joint appointment and dismissal. In this respect, our cabinet system is one of the most advanced in the whole world, and far surpasses the present German system.

The ministers of state in this country being thus appointed and dismissed conjointly, their responsibility must likewise be joint and united. Of this, clear proof is afforded by the fact that the members of the cabinet here always remain in, and retire from, office together with the Minister President.

In view of both practice and theory so far prevailing, the principle of the responsibility of ministers of state may be formulated as follows:—

For acts done by the head of a department of state of his own volition and not by virtue of resolutions passed in the cabinet, the Minister concerned alone is responsible; while for acts done pursuant of resolutions passed in the cabinet, all the ministers are conjointly responsible.

This is all the responsibility assumed by the cabinet ministers even in England — a country where the system of joint responsibility is held in greater esteem than in any other country, and where that system is regarded as the essence of constitutional government. . . .

According to the Imperial Constitution, the Emperor may, without the advice of the Minister President, appoint other ministers of state, just as he may appoint the Minister President himself without the advice of any person whomsoever. Hence the responsibility for such appointment must be assumed by the ministers so appointed, just as the responsibility for the appointment of a newly appointed Minister President would fall upon himself. The responsibility for the dismissal of a minister of state must be assumed by the minister appointed in his place and stead. Their Majesties the late and present Emperors, however, having always accepted the resignation of other ministers of state upon the advice of the Minister President, the responsibility involved necessarily fell upon the Minister President himself, and in this we find the most acceptable precedent for the purpose of preserving the unity of the cabinet.

A statesman ordered to organize a cabinet should respectfully decline to act upon such command if he considers himself unequal to the task. In the contrary case, yet if he fears the state of affairs at home and abroad will render it impossible for him to fill his office satisfactorily, he ought likewise to decline. This is but a duty or obligation which a statesman owes to his Sovereign and to his country. But if he should accept the Imperial mandate and agree to undertake the task, he must assume all the responsibility involved in his appointment to the post. To try to gag the mouth of the public against him by pleading compulsion to obey the Imperial command is the act of a man who does not realise the responsibility of a minister of state for advice and assistance, or of what a subject owes to his sovereign.

In short, notwithstanding that the Emperor's constitutional power to appoint and dismiss his cabinet ministers is such as has been detailed above, His Majesty the late Emperor invariably acted upon the recommendation of the existing or prospective Minister President, because he was deeply solicitous that constitutional government should be carried out in its essence, and because he reposed great confidence in the head of his cabinet. It would be hard to enumerate the facilities which the statesmen of this country enjoy as a result of this arrangement in carrying on the work of administration. Those who wish to act in consonance with the gracious intentions of the late Emperor should, therefore, carefully observe the precedent of joint appointment and joint responsibility, and assist in the accomplishment of the great work inaugurated by him. Those who observe and act upon the precedent of joint appointment and dismissal and yet flout the idea of joint responsibility, which is a natural corollary, or those who recognizing the principle of joint responsibility, yet do not admit its natural consequence — the formation of party government — are, I am afraid, not patterned after the heart of the late Emperor. If His Majesty had been opposed to party government, I venture to presume that he would not have left behind him, as he did, precedents of joint appointment and joint responsibility.

"It must come to pass at last:
What I purpose for the sake of my people and
  my country."
  (*A stanza by the Emperor Meiji.*)

THE PRESENT POLITICAL STAGE OF THE EMPIRE

Under the present system, military and naval men are empowered to assume any official position whatsoever in addition to those military duties which are properly attached to their profession — that is — they are qualified to be Ministers or Vice-ministers of Education, Finance, Agriculture and Commerce — branches of the administration which are removed as far as possible from things military; while at the same time, civilians are absolutely disqualified for the posts of Ministers and Vice-ministers of War and the Navy, and the Governor-General of Korea, Formosa, or Kwantung. In this manner, an inequality like that which exists between conquerors and conquered is established between civil and military officers. In the civil service, officials — other than Ministers of State — who are personally appointed by the Emperor — are so few in number that they can be counted on the fingers of both hands; but in the military service there are several scores of such, including Governors-General of various colonies, Commanders of Divisions, Commanders of Naval Stations, etc.

In view of the very nature of the official position, the Minister President [or Prime Minister] ought not only to have knowledge of all affairs of state, but the general control as well. As a matter of fact, however, military and naval officers are authorized to approach the Emperor direct upon affairs of state, and otherwise than through the medium of the Minister President, and obtain decisions thereon. For example, the project for a great expansion of the Army and Navy subsequent to the Russo-Japanese War was first resolved upon by the military and naval authorities, who then obtained approval thereof direct from the Emperor; and it was only later that the matter was referred to the Minister President. Thus, Minister President as he was in name, he had no part whatever in the decision of schemes of national defence which are intimately related to the most important of affairs of state, diplomacy and finance; but had the honour (*sic*) of being notified of the result only after the question had been finally disposed of! Besides, the War and Naval Departments issue "military ordinances," which are administrative acts unrecognized by the Constitution; (down to 1907 the matters dealt with by such ordinances were provided for by Imperial Ordinances). They have also a

Board of Marshals and Admirals of the Fleet (*Gensui-fu*) and a Military Council (*Gunji Sangi-in*), etc. — organizations which are all intended to afford special protection to the military power. These are only a few of innumerable and clear proofs evidencing the rampancy of the military clique and the inequality of the civil and military services.

From these few instances, it will be realized how the alleged equality of all classes of the people is a mere hollow phrase intended to deceive fools. And with such an unfair institutional disparity between even the civil and military services — which are alike parts of the same Government — can it be wondered that a similar state of things should exist between the bureaucracy and party politicians?

The examples quoted above merely indicate unfairness and inequality in laws and ordinances, but when we come to consider how such laws and ordinances are worked and enforced, the partiality displayed is simply astonishing. Even among those military officers (all alike recipients of special protection) those who belong to the privileged clans, or have become naturalized in them, are promoted over the heads of their equals and enjoy many other favourable distinctions, while those who have no connection with such clans have little opportunity for exhibiting their abilities, and not a few promising young officers (belonging to the latter group) are dismissed in the middle of their career. It is a reprehensible practice engendered by the long tenure of power by certain clans; and although it is gradually on the wane, yet it is far from being extinct: for what wonder is there if, after they have dared openly to set up such inequality and unfairness in the legal system despite the public gaze concentrated on them, these privileged clansmen should clandestinely bend and twist the laws to suit their own ends.

The remnants of the group of politicians representing certain clan influence have transformed themselves into a military and bureaucratic clique, their policy being to maintain by legal means the power remaining to them. The strife between the civil and military services, represented by Princes Itō and Yamagata respectively, resulted in the special protection which is legally accorded to the military clique. But when it came to a struggle between officialdom and the people, both were found on the same side and the same clan, with interests almost in common. Thus, the *Ordinance Concerning the Appointment of Civil Officials,* the *Civil Service Regulations,* etc. were enacted, and special protection was extended to persons of bureaucratic origin, while party politicians were placed in an exceedingly unfair and invidious position. I will here give just one example of the fact.

According to the present system, all officials of each Department, from the Vice-minister downwards, must be men of certain official experience. Such being the case, a party leader who may be ordered to organize a cabinet is first confronted with the difficulty of finding Ministers of War and the Navy, and then with Vice-ministers and so forth. He is thus obliged to recommend men who have for many years been supported and distinguished by the military clique as candidates for Ministers of War and the Navy, and to fill the posts of Vice-ministers downwards with men of the same class, so that a politician of party origin who finds himself at the head of a Department is a Minister of State in name only: as a matter of fact he is a veritable prisoner in the enemy's camp, his secretary being the only partizan he can trust. No matter how able such a statesman may be, what can he possibly achieve when he finds himself the solitary head of a Department with a Vice-Minister and other subordinates who have for many years received favours from his political enemy — the group of statesmen representing certain clan or bureaucratic influence, arrayed against him both in ideals and sentiment, and his only supporter in his own secretary?

A clan or bureaucratic politician, however, can fill the posts of Ministers of War and the Navy as well as those of Vice-ministers downwards with men whom he has favoured and thus endeared to himself during many years. Is not this a glaring inequality and unfairness in our institutions? And it has all been set up for the purpose of protecting certain clan influence and crushing political parties.

Such is the present state of the political stage in this country. The stage is not one which has been arranged for the statesmen of the Empire in general, but for those politicians who represent certain clan cliques and the bureaucracy, a very convenient arrangement for the latter, but a most inconvenient and disadvantageous one for the statesmen of the country at large. What I hope and struggle for is a stage on which *all* Japanese subjects can alike enjoy the same facilities.

I do not demand absolute equality between the civil and military services. These services would be on a truly equal footing if a civilian was qualified to be Chief of the General Staff or Commander of an Army, just as a military or naval officer *is* qualified to become Prime Minister, but I do not ask for this. There would be true equality between the two services were affairs of state — other than military — to be dealt with exclusively by civilians, while military affairs (as is actually the case) are left entirely in charge of military men; but I do not demand this either.

I do not object to military men having charge of affairs of state other than military, even though civilians may be excluded from any share in military affairs. All I say is that the posts of administrative chiefs and second chiefs of the Departments of War and the Navy and Governors–General of Korea, Formosa, and Kwantung should be open to civilians as well as to military men. I only maintain that the prohibitive notice board "No Admittance to Civilians" now hung up at the gates of these administrative offices should be taken down. Even though the board in question be taken down and civilians

and military men placed on an equal footing in regard to these administrative posts, it follows as a matter of course that if a military officer should be found to be the better qualified for any such post, the appointment would go to him. I only object to the fact of administrative affairs other than military being legally and exclusively in the hands of military men. . . .

THE PRESENT STATE OF POLITICAL PARTIES IN THIS COUNTRY

If the present state of political parties in this country is compared with what it was thirty odd years ago when they were first organized, the progress in organization, training, discipline and influence is extraordinary. But much is still to be desired. The following may be mentioned among the existing defects:—

(1) Little importance is attached to principles and political views;

(2) They are too deeply affected by historic and sentimental considerations;

(3) They are apt to lose sight of their main object in their eagerness to be uppermost.

(4) They are, as political parties, devoid of the sense of justice.

But these remarks of mine must not be quoted as pleas for the defence of certain clan cliques. I make them simply because I have spent all the best years of my life for the development of party government which I love deeply and sincerely, and I desire nothing better than to see its perfect realization. I freely admit that political parties have many defects, but they are few indeed compared with those of clan cliques and a bureaucracy.

I am often asked by visitors from Europe and America as to differences between the programmes of the various political parties in this country. On every occasion I feel ashamed and know not what answer to make, for what difference is there between the programmes of the Seiyūkai and the Kenseikai (the two principal parties at the present day)? It is not merely foreign visitors who are puzzled over the matter. For even the leaders of the parties themselves must find it far from easy to answer the question. Much more so must be the case with the rank and file. One party only knows how to denounce and attack the other, as if they were the foes of their own fathers, and that merely on historic and sentimental grounds. But they are not to blame for this, the fact being that there is no clear distinction between the party programmes. Not only is there no clear distinction between them, but in desiring to pull down the clan clique and establish party government, the object and interests of both parties have always been identical. But they cannot take common action even for this common object; they have alternately joined forces with their enemy and attacked each other, pursuing as they do a common object, and thus the clan clique has profited by their internal strife. The two great parties in this country have — from the time they were known as *Jiyūtō* (Liberals) and *Kaishintō* (Progressionists) to this day, when they bear the names of *Seiyūkai* and *Kenseikai* respectively, that is, for the long period of thirty-six or seven years — invariably repeated this foolish proceeding, and that is the reason why, — by skilfully playing them one against the other — even now that the influence of certain clans has largely decreased, the clique still contrives to retain power in its own hands. Should the two parties take common action for the achievement of common objects, it would be the easiest thing in the world for them to crush the clan clique and inaugurate a new era of party government. After the remnant of that clique has been driven out and a fair and equal political stage erected, the two parties may compete under the banner of their respective fixed principles and views, the fittest winning the day and the less fit losing it, the winners to go in and form a cabinet according to Imperial command, while the defeated retire and plan schemes for resuming the fight. Is not that a manly task for manly men? How much wiser and more advantageous, beyond comparison, will it be for the parties to act in such a way instead of alternately taking sides with the clan politicians and weakening the very foundation of political parties?

. . . Here in the Orient we have had the conception of a faction; but none of a public party. A political party is an association of people having for its exclusive object the discussion of public affairs of state and the enforcement of their views thereon. But when political parties are transplanted into the East, they at once partake of the nature of factions, pursuing private and personal interests instead of the interests of the state — as witnessed by the fact of their joining hands by turns with the clan cliques or using the construction of railways, ports and harbours, schools, etc. as means for extending party influence. Besides, the customs and usages of feudal times are so deeply impressed upon the minds of men here that even the idea of political parties, as soon as it enters the brains of our countrymen, germinates and grows according to feudal notions. Such being the case, even political parties, which should be based and dissolved solely on principle and political views, are really affairs of personal connections and sentiments, the relations between the leader and the members of a party being similar to those which subsisted between a feudal lord and his liegemen, or to those between a "boss" of gamblers and his followers in this country. A politician scrupulous enough to join or desert a party for the sake of principle is denounced as a political traitor or renegade. That political faith should be kept not *vis-à-vis* its leader or its officers but *vis-à-vis* its principles and views is not understood. They foolishly think that the proverb "*A Faithful servant never serves two masters: a chaste wife never sees two husbands*" is equally applicable to the members of a political party. In their erroneous opinion, it is a loyal act on the part of a member of a party to change his principles and views in accordance with orders from headquarters, while in the event of headquarters changing their views it is unfaithful to desert them. . . . The ideas governing the relations between a feudal lord and his vassals, or those between a chief of gamblers and his following, call for blind obedience to commands without regard to right or wrong or good or evil. No wonder that trained and disciplined by such a conception, a political party should be turned into a personal faction, and devote itself exclusively to the extension of its own influence, heedless of principles and views!

. . . [I]s it in the nature of things that a political party, acting in accordance with the dictate of principles, should, when transplanted to the Orient, become a personal faction which pays no special regard to principles and views? There are among members of a party many who strenuously denounce any assistance rendered to another party by prefectural governors and other officials, but defend the practice when directed for the benefit of their own party. Think of the danger of having the affairs of state controlled by men whose mental attitude is so unfair! Political parties are, however, organized out of the nation: no party can exist apart from the nation. So

if they are defective, it shows there are defects in the nation itself. If the nation is rich in political wisdom and virtue, it will be impossible for bad political parties to continue long in existence. While the voters inflicted a severe blow upon the Seiyūkai at the general election of 1915, they dealt a signal blow at the opposite party at the general election two years later, and enabled the Seiyūkai to regain much of its lost ground. The only apparent reason for this is that at the time of the former election the Seiyūkai was in the opposition, while in the latter it was on the side of the Government; and from this fact, it will be seen what a hold the idea of slavish respect for the Government and contempt for the people (*Kanson mimpi no shisō*) still retains over the mind of the nation. It is small wonder that political parties, as well as other institutions and bodies, should have failed to achieve any marked development. At this rate, the realization of constitutional government seems to lie in the dim and distant future.

"How long the days and months appear to one,
When working and waiting for the accomplishment of one's cherished purpose."
(*A stanza by the Emperor Meiji.*)

Universal Suffrage Seen as the Antidote
to Big Money Elections (1924)

TSURUMI YŪSUKE

To Constitutional limitations and feudalistic factionalism should be added the extraordinary cost of elections as another handicap in the way of developing parliamentary democracy in prewar Japan. This problem was acutely analyzed by Tsurumi Yūsuke, an aspiring politician who, after graduating from Tōkyō Imperial University, entered the Ministry of Railways. He resigned in 1924 and traveled to the United States to give lectures opposing the 1923 Immigration Law which excluded Japanese. This selection is taken from a lecture he gave at Yale University during that trip. He was then still unsullied by political life, but he was well aware of the financial problems involved in politics. He thought that the enactment of universal suffrage could "clean up" Japanese politics. Actually election costs became even greater.

Tsurumi's later career was typical of many Japanese prewar "liberals." Upon returning to Japan, he attacked the outdated liberalism of the two main parties, the Seiyukai and the Minseitō, and helped organize the Meiseikai as a third party. He was elected to the House of Representatives in 1928. For a while he held a casting vote as leader of the third party but then "compromised" with the Tanaka cabinet and thereby lost the trust of many of his liberal friends. Gradually he became more nationalistic. He joined the Minseitō in 1936 and was recommended by the wartime Tōjō government as a safe candidate in 1942. After the war, he was purged by the Occupation Forces, but returned to politics and held several important cabinet posts subsequently.

Now I come to an explanation of the way in which the constitutional machine established in 1889 has operated to hold down the pressure of liberal forces.

First of all, of course, is the limited suffrage, which gives Japan an electorate of about three million voters, notwithstanding the recent extension of the franchise. The great mass of laborers and members of the lower middle class are deprived of the ballot altogether.

Even with this handicap, the politics of Japan would have been far more liberal had it not been for the enormous expenses involved in parliamentary elections. In explaining Japanese politics we arrive at this or start from this. The cost of elections presents one of the most perplexing problems confronting Japan today, and it is necessary for me to lay considerable emphasis on this part of my subject.

When voting was introduced it was a great novelty and few people knew anything about Western election methods. In the first campaign of 1890, election expenses were almost nothing. For example, the noted scholar Nishi was returned from the city of Okayama with the entire outlay

From Sir Valentine Chirol, Yusuke Tsurumi, and Sir James Arthur Salter, *The Reawakening of the Orient and Other Addresses* (New Haven, 1925), pp. 75–85. Published for the Institute of Politics. Reprinted by permission of Yale University Press.

of one yen, or fifty cents in American money. This was the amount he spent for his transportation in a rickshaw from his village to Okayama. But according to a conservative estimate for the election of last May, candidates spent on the average 50,000 yen. The maximum is said to have been 400,000 yen. Cases of 200,000 yen are not very rare. The minimum record is that of Mr. Inukai, the leader of the Kakushin Club or Reform Club, who has been returned unopposed since the opening of the Diet. He makes no campaign; he just sends letters of thanks to every voter after election; this costs him something like one thousand yen.

This extraordinary cost of elections is the curse of Japanese politics and some of our greatest political evils are traced to this one outstanding cause. By concentrating our attention on this single fact, we can understand the real political situation of present-day Japan very clearly.

Let us study the effects this has brought in its train.

1. In the first place, the necessity of great outlays has had a decisive influence on the character of candidates for Parliament. It has practically shut the door of the House to the middle class and also to the laboring people. Independent men who do not care to give pledges to their rich friends have found it impossible to get into political life. Some have managed somehow to raise expenses for one or two elections, but could not last long. There are cases of downright tragedy; the master of many a well-to-do family has gone into politics with sincere, patriotic motives and ruined not only his own career, but also the life of his whole family. To run for a seat in the House sends cold shudders through the hearts of the candidate's family and friends in Japan.

2. In the second place, the high cost of elections naturally means that money is the primary requisite of a candidate. His principles and personality have very little to do with his success in the election. It has a most lamentable effect on the quality of the House of Representatives; having very few strong men, its prestige declined. The decline of the lower house in the people's eyes gave an unduly large share of power to the upper house and also to the bureaucracy.

3. There is, in the third place, a singular feature in Japanese politics which arises from expensive elections. It is the fear, or I should say dread, of dissolution on the part of the M.P.'s. Being in a hard-earned position, costing so much, they tremble at the thought of dissolution. This psychology was capitalized on by unscrupulous politicians. The Government has the full power to dissolve the House by getting the Emperor's sanction. So, holding this sword above the heads of M.P.'s, it can force almost any number of unpalatable measures on the unwilling members.

This, to my mind, is one of the chief reasons for the great power of the Genro. I should like to avail myself of this opportunity and explain the nature of the world-famous Genro, or elder statesmen of Japan.

The Genro have no official status. Their position has been due to peculiar political conditions of Japan. The late Emperor Meiji used to summon a council of his trusted subjects outside the cabinet to confer with cabinet ministers on grave questions of state. Particularly when a premier resigned and no successor was found, the counsel of these elder statesmen was deemed necessary. The function of the Genro gradually narrowed down to the selection of a new premier.

The selection of a premier is rather simple in such countries as England or France. A man who is supposed to have the support of the majority of the lower house of Parliament is the one to organize a cabinet. However, it is not so simple in Japan. One reason is that the whole political power is not concentrated in the lower house, but a greater reason is, in my opinion, because a new premier has the absolute power to dissolve the House and by skillful maneuvers can elect a majority of his own. Okuma in 1915 dissolved the House and won a tremendous majority. Terauchi in 1917 dissolved the House and again won a great majority. I am inclined to attribute the defeat of Kiyoura this year not to his unpopularity, but rather to his weakness in management and lack of political adroitness.

Such being the situation, the Genro have had quite a wide field for the selection of premiers. It has not been necessary for them to recommend the leader of the majority party or the leader of the opposition. They have been able to select practically any man who could by any process organize a cabinet. Therefore when a cabinet crisis comes the attention of the nation is concentrated on the Genro.

This makes the Genro's position rather strong. A man ambitious to be premier must be careful not to incur their displeasure. This also accounts for the conservative nature of Japanese politics. When Yamagata was alive, he was practically the whole Genro. He could make and unmake a cabinet. But since his death, early in 1922, the power of the Genro has gradually waned. There is only Prince Saionji left, and, in the face of the changing social conditions, he will find it more and more difficult to impose his own will upon the nation. I think I am pretty safe in predicting that with Prince Saionji the last of the Genro will pass away.

Then Japan will doubtless resort to the English system of having the outgoing premier recommend the incoming premier. . . .

4. There is another effect of the abnormally large election expenses, *i.e.*, the unavoidable need of every M.P. to recover the money he spent during the campaign. Every M.P. cannot be expected to be a good business man. Hence the unsavory dealings which constitute a great evil of Japan. Corruption during the campaign means corruption after it. The famous sugar scandal of 1910 is a grievous instance.

In all fairness to my own countrymen, I must also tell you that there are a number of sincere reformers who, under heavy disadvantages, have been fighting all these evils, and, thanks to their efforts, brighter days are expected to come.

I must briefly explain here the causes that brought about this unwholesome condition in Japanese politics.

The first and the greatest responsibility falls on the shoulders of the people themselves. They were in the beginning entirely unaccustomed to voting. Therefore they voted as the local bosses told them to; and this created a deplorable situation, namely, the dominance of a class of people who make it their business to organize political machines and squeeze money out of candidates. More blame is to be laid at the door of the educators. They did not give the necessary civic education to the people.

The second reason is more personal. I think the statesmen of Meiji are to be blamed. Yamagata must shoulder a great deal of responsibility for his unscrupulous methods in dealing with party men. Some party leaders were not faultless. Men like Hoshi and Hara cannot escape the reproach of fair critics for their Machiavellian method of promoting party interests.

In the third place, defects in the election law must also be cited. Under the existing law, the control of elections is under the Home Minister, the prefectural governors and the police. It is there that political considerations enter. A new law is under consideration to increase the power of the judiciary so as to make bribing impossible during elections.

However, minute changes in the law of procedure will not be effective in doing away with the political evils which I have just enumerated. The cause lies deeper and the remedy is to come from another source. These great political evils, in my opinion, flowed from the failure of the Meiji Restoration to cultivate the germs of liberalism that sprang up and could not be utterly stamped out by any process. The statesmen of that period restored the Imperial House; they created a strong central government; they saved Japan from falling under foreign domination; but they neg-

lected to emancipate the people. They
failed to foresee and prepare for the coming of democracy when they abolished
feudal tenures, established a parliament,
and made provision for universal education. They ruled the country; they gave
the middle class practically no share in
the Government; they gave far less to labor.
It is by emancipating the middle and working classes that the system of faction and
corruption that is so powerful in Japanese
politics can be broken down. . . .

The coming of the remedy is inevitable.
It is at hand. The World War, which
really brought about an industrial revolution in Japan, created a large, prosperous,
and independent middle class and called
into being an active labor movement that
cannot be stayed or turned. When the
storm broke in August, 1914, Japan little
dreamed what a great effect it was destined
to have upon her. A temporary business depression was soon followed by a sudden
boom and in 1915 practically every fac-
tory was humming with work and more
work. Coincidently with the material
change came another one no less marked.
It was the change in political and social
ideas.

The new spirit that was gaining ground
both in Europe and America rushed into
the Island Empire like an avalanche; democracy and liberty were much on the lips
of the people. Speeches of the European
and American statesmen on the Allied side
were followed with intense interest. Mr.
[Theodore] Roosevelt and Mr. Lloyd
George never failed to arouse enthusiasm.
Speeches and messages of President Wilson
reached the farthest corners of the Empire.

The liberals at home were not idle. Men
like Professors Nitobe and Yoshino were
active in disseminating the idea of democracy. The conservatives were frightened
and tried to thwart the cause by stamping
on it a peculiar brand of "dangerous
thoughts." But they little realized that far
more dangerous thoughts were being
brewed by the changing social conditions

namely, violent socialism and anarchism.
By persecuting those who cherished sane
ideas of liberalism and democracy, they
were driving sensitive, subtle minds further towards the radical cause. . . .

The newspapers of the country, with
very few exceptions, were on the side of
democracy. They, of course, reflected the
intellectual currents flowing among the
people. Japan in the later years of the
World War seemed to make a fair stride
towards liberalism and democracy. The
prosperous middle class became bolder, and
the conservative ruler seemed on the ebbing
tide. The sagacious Yamagata was wise
enough to read the signs of the times, and
was apparently withdrawing his tentacles.

The failure of the democratic leaders of
the early days may be traced to many
causes. But the predominant reason is . . .
the lack of popular support . . . [T]hose
leaders were mostly men who had private axes to grind. They were mainly
samurai of Tokugawa affiliations or those
of the Tosa and Hizen clans, and they belonged to the same class they fought
against. The people found very few economic or moral reasons for supporting them
enthusiastically. They were rather in sympathy with the conservatives, who gave
them national security and economic prosperity.

But the rising tide of the new liberalism
at the end of the World War had an entirely different significance. In the first
place, it came from the people. The spread
of education gave them more power to
think and to understand. Economic prosperity gave them more independence. The
increasing power of big capital, the accu-
mulation of which was speeded up by the
World War, impressed upon them the
vague need of defending themselves by
popular representation against the oligarchic rule of the statesmen and big business men and industrialists. . . .

The intellectual currents were running
even faster than the actual accomplishments in the field of politics. Some sar-
castic foreign critics called it Japan's "lip

service" to liberalism; but men like Ozaki and Yoshino were exposed to personal risks more than once in pleading for their cause. Some even went to prison for their bold utterances. . . .

These liberal tendencies are now converging on a definite point—that is, universal manhood suffrage. It is an issue on which the liberalism of Japan is going to have a test. It is quite out of place to tell you all about the conflicts of forces in the past four years. But it is quite probable that the suffrage bill will pass both houses of the Parliament and will become law next winter. That would mean a great stride towards democracy. Japanese internal politics would take on a new phase.

Political Parties Seen as
the Sine Qua Non for Democracy (1932)

HAROLD S. QUIGLEY

From 1925, when manhood suffrage was passed, to 1932 which saw the end of "party rule" with the assassination of Premier Inukai, three general elections for the Diet were held: in 1928, 1930, and 1932. During this period, the first American political scientist to write a textbook on Japanese government was studying the political scene. After doing his graduate work at the University of Wisconsin, Dr. Quigley received fellowships enabling him to visit Japan four times — in 1921, 1923, 1930, and 1931, the third time during a general election — before making the following observations.

It was his view at the time that, bad as they were, parties constituted a *sine qua non* for the emergence of true democratic government, a stage which he did not think Japan had yet reached. But just as his book came out in 1932, the last of the "party cabinets" fell.

Dilemmas implicit in his observations: How can the parties become more responsible when the Diet has such limited powers? And yet how can the Diet gain more powers unless through the development of strong, responsible parties? Also, how can the parties promote democracy, when they are so undemocratic internally — including the labor parties?

F IRST-HAND observation of the functioning of the Seiyukai and the Minseito, Japan's major political parties, supports this primary conclusion drawn from the brief survey of their history that is possible here: they are effective organizations for the accomplishment of the purposes to which the existing constitutional system limits the instrumentalities of a democratic order. They have overwhelmed the theory of a government independent of the Diet by deadlocking legislation and by winning the goodwill of the people. "Transcendentalism" may still be destined to enjoy brief interludes of power, but party cabinets may fairly be assumed to have become the established rule. Party cabinets and party government are not as yet, however, synonymous terms in Japan. Far-reaching constitutional changes which will permit the Diet

From Harold S. Quigley, *Japanese Government and Politics: An Introductory Study* (New York, 1932), pp. 232–236 and 245–246. Reprinted by permission of Harold S. Quigley.

to assume the rôle of lawgiver, and which await the fuller awakening of the people to the implications of their political rights, must precede the realization of party government. These changes will come as the advances already made have come — out of the abrasive action of party politics upon the hard flint of the oligarchy that was and is Japan.

Japanese parties are products of absentee ancestry and an unfriendly environment. They were imitations of Western parties and were inaugurated by the clan leaders Okuma and Itagaki in the period of transition from feudalism to constitutionalism. Thus it is but natural that they should exhibit the marks of their birth and breeding. The readiness of the Jiyuto to accept the leadership of Ito in 1900, and of a large section of the Kokuminto to enroll in the Doshikai under Katsura in 1913, was consistent with Japanese, if not with Occidental, conceptions of political procedure. As recently as 1926, the Seiyukai found it convenient to elect the head of the Choshu clan [Tanaka Giichi] to the presidency of the party. It is more than probable that both the major parties will be headed by important clansmen in the future.

This relationship not only prolongs the influence of an ultraconservative aristocracy beyond the epoch of history to which it belonged; it sets the mode for the attitude to be observed between party leaders outside the aristocracy and in the rank and file of party membership. Hara and Inukai, Kato and Hamaguchi were as dominant over their parties as were Ito and Okuma. Political bosses — sometimes as party presidents, sometimes as advisers — exert an influence even greater than that of the men behind the scenes in American party life. This is an unhealthy state of things, however able and liberal the leaders may be. It frustrates the growth of popular participation in party life and in government, the very purposes for which political parties were established. It gives the aspect of military combat to party relations, itensifying rivalry and encouraging the use of repre-

hensible tactics inside and outside the Diet. It postpones the realization of cabinet responsibility to the popular chamber by exalting the leaders of the parties, who take advantage of their position to "railroad" legislation and to accomplish by ordinance objects properly within the statutory field. Undoubtedly the rise of commoners to the seats of power monopolized until 1918 by the nobility was a noteworthy step toward popular government.

Japanese parties profess to be devoted to liberal principles, but, like their prototypes in the West, they cannot exist without funds, and this unhappy circumstance forces them into alliances, similar to those familiar in America and Europe, with great business and industrial corporations. Thus to one type of master, the clan, is added a second, the economic group representing accumulated capital. These masters sometimes exhibit interests that clash, and a cabinet elected by the Mitsubishi trust may fall before the attack of the Privy Council. Certainly, between serving two such impatient masters and serving the people by whose suffrages they were elected, members of the House of Representatives are likely to find the former obligation the more pressing. For this situation, as for its parallel (minus the aristocracy) in the United States, there is no apparent remedy that is peculiar to Japan.

A third characteristic in the party life of Japan is the peculiar combination of a high degree of loyalty to a leader with a low degree of loyalty to the party itself. Members pass readily from one party to another; there are frequent breaches between factions within a party, followed by splits and the formation of new groups which may later merge with the opposition. Old parties assume new names in order to attract members. These changes are at times the result of bribery, at times due to anticipated official preferment, rarely to agreements or disagreements on points of principle. The ever-present possibility of such moves is a retarding influence in the uphill struggle of the parties with the antagonistic traditions and agencies of oligarchical rule.

The parties reveal the scars of this half-century struggle. The continuous interference of the government with freedom of speech, the press, and assemblage has frightened liberals and hindered the up-building of a larger popular membership. It has intensified rancor between the "ins" and the "outs" and stimulated rowdyism and bribery during elections. Cabinets of a partisan composition are glad to make use of oligarchical tactics against the opposition, tactics for which they can assert warrant in imperial prerogatives. This tendency is maintained, it would seem, principally because of the dependence of the cabinet upon surviving oligarchical controls like the Privy Council, the genro, the Imperial Household Ministry, and the supreme command, but also because party men in cabinet offices are dominated by the permanent civil service, which is highly bureaucratic. Many of them are ex-bureaucrats themselves, imbued with traditional ideals.

It is an encouraging fact that the conservative and imperialist Seiyukai, which dominated the House of Representatives and was allied with the Choshu clan from 1900 to 1914 and from 1916 to 1924, now faces a vigorous equal in the more liberal and internationalist Minseito. The latter party is responsible for the enactment of manhood suffrage, for partial reform of the House of Peers, and for ratification of the London Naval Treaty. It is intent upon extending the suffrage to women, enacting proportional representation for the lower house of the Diet, and granting a favorable legal status to labor-unions. The remarkable popular support of the Minseito is evidence of the growth of democratic consciousness, which the Seiyukai cannot afford to ignore. These facts render less significant the debacle that overtook the so-called liberal group, the Meiseikai.

Perhaps the most frequently read criticism of Japanese parties is that their platforms are vague to the point of vacuity.

General principles rather than specific items of programs of action have indeed composed the platforms. Dependent as they have been while in office upon forces which they cannot control, party leaders have been opposed to platforms pledging them to actions which they may find themselves unable to perform. Thus the policies of a party are discoverable in the proposals for legislation that are made during its tenure of the government and, to a smaller degree, in its attitude while in opposition toward the government's proposals. The continued conservatism of the Japanese people is reflected in all the non-proletarian parties; nevertheless it is not difficult, as above noted, to discern a relative liberalism in the Minseito; and certain of the smaller groups, such as the Kokumin Doshikai and the Kakushinto, profess even more liberal doctrines.

It is the favorite cry of liberals in Japan to-day that the parties are effete, corrupt, quarrelsome, selfish — in general disreputable and deserving of reproach. Granted the truth of these criticisms, what was to be expected from the materials with which the parties have had to build and in the presence of the obstacles, constitutional and administrative, with which they have had to contend? *Politician* has not been a savory term in Japan; it has suggested all the unpleasant attributes of the parvenu in addition to those of the spoils-man. The parties have no roots in the past, whereas their opponents in the bureaucratic hierarchy have a rootage of many centuries' growth. However, no agencies other than the parties exist to fight the people's battles. Without them, bad as they are, return to feudalism would be inevitable. It is, therefore, the part of reformers not to seek to destroy party life but to bring about such a modification of the old order of things that there may be room for party activity to expand, for greater responsibilities to induce a higher sense of responsibility, for popular influence to find fearless expression — in short for democratic government to replace the present reign of privilege. What parties are to-day is not a gauge of what they may become, either in Japan or in the United States, from which, regrettably, some of the less desirable features of Japanese party politics have been borrowed. . . .

*   *   *

OBSERVATIONS ON THE PROLETARIAN
OR LABOR PARTIES

The causes of disunion among the labor parties are many. One notable consideration is the fact that there are differences of opinion upon methods of political action which do not appear in the statements of platforms because of the attitude of the government and the extreme penalties provided in the peace preservation law against anything savoring of radicalism. This explains the mutual suspicion that is manifested between the Ronoto [the "new" Labor Farmer Party, the most radical of the legal proletarian parties] and the other [labor] parties. Between and within the parties which accept parliamentarism, disunity is promoted by the type of their leadership,

which is principally that of theorists rather than of men of actual experience in the world of labor. This factor is strengthened by the continued weakness of the Diet, which renders mutual abnegation of pet ideas in favor of a pragmatic program unlikely to be fruitful.

Other obstacles to labor coöperation [and therefore to the effectiveness of the proletarian parties in representing the interests of labor, the tenant farmers, and poorer classes generally] are the jealousy that exists between the leaders, who allow personal feelings to affect their decisions on matters of policy; the ambitions which prompt leaders to prefer dominance over a small faction to a lesser place in a larger organization; and lack of funds and of political experience under a régime of increased individualism in which feudal authority should be replaced by agreement. As in the older parties, there is a marked inclination to perpetuate the feudal relationship of lord and vassal between the leaders and the rank and file of the labor groups.

The Inability of Japanese Capitalism
to Make Democracy a Success

ROBERT A. SCALAPINO

The very timing and tempo of the industrial revolution in Japan provides for Dr. Scalapino of the Political Science Department of the University of California at Berkeley the key to failure of democracy in prewar Japan.

By the latter half of the nineteenth century the advanced industrial nations were carving out spheres of influence abroad. With the opening of Japan to foreign intercourse in 1853, the Japanese were faced with the prospects of either falling into the sphere of influence of one of the great powers or growing strong enough to prevent this. As a result, the considerations of national defense were more important than free competition in the development of the basic industries in Japan. Instead of producing a business middle class that employed democratic slogans of civil liberties to prevent government interference, capitalism in Japan spawned zaibatsu (financial clique) interests that depended heavily on government and sought to influence it in various ways. Simultaneously a mass of small businesses proliferated, competing fiercely among themselves with very little capital at their disposal. The latter did not gain much political influence, but the former could sway and even corrupt the political parties with their great wealth. This brought opprobrium on the parliamentary process, in which, in any case, big business did not feel it had a great stake. Dr. Scalapino skillfully traces out the various ways this central fact undermined the democratic forces in prewar Japan.

To explore the most vital aspect of party failure in its unfolding, and also to cast light upon the remarkable strength of antidemocratic institutions in Japan, special attention must be given to the political role of modern Japanese capitalism. Out of the Meiji Restoration emerged two formidable pressure groups, the landowners and the urban business classes. Much of the chronicle of the leading parties must be written in terms of their political propensities, and since these were connected with the socioeconomic forces developing within and outside Japanese society, some brief examination of these forces must be undertaken, with particular emphasis upon the rise of Japanese industrialism.

. . . At the outset of constitutional government, . . . the industrial revolution had only begun to unfold. In the recent background was a record of feverish governmental activities, the overcoming of certain political and economic obstacles, and the beginnings of an expansion of private enterprise. In the future there was to be an incredibly rapid development in all these directions. Its first phases unfolded in the decade between 1885 and 1895, a period in which further progress in meeting fiscal, technical, and supply problems resulted in significant advances in capital investment and industrial production. . . .

Old trends continued and new ones were initiated in the next decade, from 1895 to

From Robert A. Scalapino, *Democracy and the Party Movement in Prewar Japan: The Failure of the First Attempt* (Berkeley, 1953), pp. 247–255, 266, 268–274, 276 and 290–293. Reprinted by permission of the University of California Press.

1905. This period, sandwiched between two successful wars, was marked by substantial increases in industrial capitalization and in foreign trade, the strengthening of policies of aid by the government, and the mechanization of new fields. . . .

In order to place the political limitations of late Meiji capitalism in perspective, some recapitulation of its antecedents is necessary. It had emerged hastily and at a comparatively late date in the midst of an unprepared society, and therefore its development was initially dependent upon intensive government planning, supervision, and subsidization. Subsequently, beginning with the 1880's outright state capitalism receded in favor of private enterprise sustained against domestic weaknesses and foreign threats by a neomercantilist policy. Such a transition was in accordance with the desires of the early Meiji political leaders, whose chief energies had been directed toward utilizing all methods of rapid industrial expansion.

This pattern of development, together with the prior traditions which supported and were supported by it, was vitally important in shaping the personnel, structure, and philosophy of modern Japanese capitalism. We have already noted that one product was the large number of new industrial leaders who were men of the old bushi class and consequently men whose political predilections and personal friendships — not to mention economic security — lay with the government. With Meiji political and economic elites extremely small in numbers, with the latter frequently selected by the former and having a similar background, close personalized contacts were most natural. At the same time, however, these were ordinarily not contacts between "equals," despite changes in the official attitude toward business. The social stigma attached to commercialism was not to be cast off lightly, and this, supplemented by the very great obligations of commerce and industry to government, tended to produce strong notes of apology and deference in the attitude of the business class toward public officials. Even ex-bushi members, frequently affected by inner pangs of remorse or chagrin at a status which conflicted with the tenets of their own past philosophy, and heavily dependent upon political support, tended to find simultaneous release from psychological and economic insecurity by assuming the subservient role. These inclinations were of course much stronger among the ex-commoner elements of the new business world and were slow to diminish, especially in the first generation.

In structure, as well, industrial capitalism reflected in graphic form the nature of its development and certain characteristics of its political impact. The keynote of Japanese industry was centralization, with the ultimate financial-economic controls held by the government and a few powerful groups known popularly as *zaibatsu* (financial cliques). Although small and medium businesses occupied a far more important position in over-all production than has generally been recognized, as we shall have occasion to note later, still, in the final analysis, their position was one of great dependency upon zaibatsu and government. And in many basic fields, moreover, the tendencies toward oligopoly were pronounced, only rarely challenged, and usually progressive, with cartelization developing toward the end of the Meiji period. There are undoubtedly many factors which enter into an explanation for these characteristics; the paucity of capital, the lack of adequate resources, and the shortage of trained personnel constituted barriers to internal competition or a broad productive base. Selectivity and an avoidance of duplication or waste were doubly important as considerations of governmental aid, given the premium on speed and the pressures of foreign competition. But perhaps it is most significant that the governmental policy of neomercantilism was applied at a time when industrial techniques were sufficiently advanced in the world to permit the structure based on this policy to be quickly established throughout the entire economy, and with a scope and tenacity which defied fundamental alteration.

Thus the zaibatsu were leading actors in the industrial-financial scene, symbols of Japanese capitalism, and ultimate recipients of tremendous economic and political power. The term zaibatsu, like most epithets, has been applied without too much regard for discrimination. [Some scholars] would divide the zaibatsu into three general groups: those whose activities centered in the finance and banking field, including Yasuda, Kawasaki, and Shibuzawa; those whose activities were industry-centered, such as Asano and Okura; and those whose activities spread into all fields — finance, commerce, and light and heavy industry — of which group Mitsui, Mitsubishi, and Sumitomo were the outstanding examples. Generally, these last three and Yasuda were considered the big four zaibatsu. Among the so-called zaibatsu, large or small, however, there were many variations and changes of organization, operational plans, and political activities. The term zaibatsu was even applied on occasion to district capitalists, with reference to their local control. Moreover, the emergence of new groups after World War I, and particularly after the rise of the military about 1932, constituted a further complication.

In spite of the intricacies of the situation, however, the increasing influence of a few great industrial and financial concerns in collaboration with the government became a vital part of the unfolding Japanese economy. Time served to separate the zaibatsu prototypes further from small and medium business, both in size and in power, and to increase the dependence of the latter upon the former. Almost down to the Russo-Japanese War, however, the economic position of the zaibatsu was quite uncertain, and their political role was generally marked by great caution; quite as much as the elements representing smaller business, they were supplicants at the government door, seeking protection, cultivating political friends, carefully repaying obligations, and accepting subordination. In these regards, Meiji zaibatsu set a tone of behavior for lesser lights in the business world and exemplified the general position of the industrial-commercial class.

Out of the general circumstances affecting business came a philosophy which carried important political implications. There is much justice in portraying the newly emerging businessmen as among the most Westernized and "enlightened" elements of Japanese society. Many businessmen had been abroad, and some had been educated in the Occident. Admiration for Western industrial techniques, Western education, and Western friends represented a new stimulus, challenging to the old order. Still, there were powerful factors operating within Japanese society to alter or confine these influences. The conjunction of nationalism and the industrialization drive, together with the world circumstances which a weak Japan faced, imposed upon the business groups a unique sense of their functional purpose as defined by the political leaders. In a period of succeeding crises, and with the voice of government constantly imploring unity and the creation of state power, the Meiji business class was ever mindful of the national goals; business enterprises even became a patriotic venture calling for unremitting zeal and wholehearted conformity to the purposes of the time. In this atmosphere there was a natural tendency to accept the supremacy of political and military leadership. . . .

Probably of greatest significance in molding the philosophy of the early modern business class, however, was the extraordinary dependency upon governmental support and the consequent reluctance to attack the power or purposes of the state. Thus, out of an inferiority complex, an ingrained nationalism, a lack of modern political experience, and a rational appraisal of their own economic interests came a philosophy which supported neomercantilism, abjured open political action, and sought to confine political activities to behind-the-scenes operations which would involve the least risks and promise the greatest rewards.

The second major factor to be discussed in analyzing the political nature of the Meiji industrial-commercial elements was the collective power of the agrarian propertied groups. What the landowners lacked in concentrated wealth or state priorities they made up in votes. The rural-urban cleavage has run very deep in modern Japan. . . . Despite the breadth of the conflict, however, in the Meiji era, the open political struggle was primarily confined to the rural landowner and urban business groups. Within their respective categories, these were naturally the more articulate elements. They had the power and the vote. And the burning economic issues such as taxation, subsidization, and price policy were ones in which they had a great stake. Although the administration often sought to harmonize the interests of these two important segments of Japanese society, neither it nor the parties could fully reconcile all the divergencies nor maintain perfectly balanced policies.

With the advent of constitutional government, the potency of the landed elements in the parties and in the representative branch of government was assured; in numbers and voting strength, they were far ahead of the urban industrial-commercial groups. The landowners, indeed, were the backbone of the Jiyuto, and without some agrarian support, no party could be more than a minor fragment. A sampling of properly spaced early elections can easily illustrate this point. In the first election of 1890, of the 300 elected members of the Diet, 129 represented the agrarian landed class directly, whereas only 19 came from the commercial and industrial classes. . . .

Thus, in the period ending about the time of the Russo-Japanese War, three tendencies in the early capitalist impact upon Japanese politics and parties can be noted. Clearly, the new business community was serving as a unifying force for party-bureaucratic alliances. If these were

generally alliances which combined the more "enlightened" or "probusiness" officials with similar elements in the parties, still, they produced basic perversions of liberal philosophy and action; . . . the resulting damage to the party movement is difficult to exaggerate. Also, it was the fate of the business elements — large and small — to be cast in the role of great corruptive influences in the political scene. Although the worst in this respect was probably yet to come, even at this point, political corruption touched every major party and many party leaders, as well as many groups within the bureaucracy. Finally, the influence which business was having on the general tenor of Japanese politics was as much the product of its weakness as of its strength. During this period the Japanese business world took a relatively limited part in political activities as a whole, and one characterized chiefly by indifference and inaction, together with a general attitude of subserviency. Concentrating upon other tasks, operating under traditional handicaps, and greatly dependent upon the government, business was, as a rule, exceedingly careful to shun the political limelight. By the end of the period, however, there were signs that some changes were occurring in the political status and activities of the business elements. A somewhat greater degree of self-confidence was creeping into the psychology of the industrial-commercial class. . . .

. . . It is probably no exaggeration to say that the period from 1905 to 1920 marked the real transition in Japan from an agrarian to an industry-centered economy. . . .

Under these circumstances it was natural that the political power and influence of the business community would spurt forward. Connected with the growth of the economic position of business was an increasing awareness of importance and authority; higher education, especially when obtained abroad, was nurturing these feelings. Moreover, the walls of agrarian supremacy were cracking wide open, and the political pressure of even its strongest representatives was showing less potency. In addition, Western science and technology were now making profound impressions upon nearly the whole of Japanese society. That this was the age of technology had never been clearer than in the crucial years of World War I; a greater acceptance of industrialization and a glorification of its accomplishments in Japan strengthened the prestige and influence of its leaders.

The future of Japanese democracy and of the party movement, however, was connected with the degree to which increased business power would be used on behalf of democratic theory and practice, as well as with the capacity which Japanese capitalism could show for coping with the problems of its society. It has been a favorite thesis among some Japanese and Western writers that the Japanese business class in this new period took up the cudgels vigorously for liberalism and led the struggle for Western-style democracy until overwhelmed by other forces. The evidence already presented should cast some doubt upon this concept; at the same time, however, one must recognize the substantial transition taking place in the position, prestige, and power of the business elements, portending possible changes in their political role. Actually, the thesis mentioned above, like most powerful myths, has within it certain elements of truth. With the possible exception of the "intellectuals," business as a class was of all Japanese groups the one that knew most about Western democracy and was most sympathetic toward it. Education and, in many cases, international contacts and interests, developed in business circles a strong cosmopolitan sense and an awareness of the philosophic proclivities of the West. The period around the First World War was one characterized by the rise of democratic sentiment everywhere. And the restraints inherent in Japanese paternalism became somewhat more irritating to men of the business world as their sense of power increased. Especially when government

threatened to engage in activities which they considered injurious to their interests did the industrial-commercial groups protest with increasing vigor. Incipient in this resistance was an element of laissez faire, which in similar forms had gone hand in hand with nineteenth-century democracy. Indeed, concomitant with this protest in Japan was a drive for greater recognition and representation, reflective in some degree of Western democratic trends, and one of its most logical means of expression was through the parties; there can be no doubt that the party movement found growing support during this period from important segments of business.

When all this has been said, however, it must be emphasized that the forces counteracting this tendency were even more compelling. Not even in the "new era" did the nearest Japanese equivalents to the Western middle class find it possible, as a group, to accept the basic tenets of democracy without major equivocation. The growth of the democratic creed among members of this class was stifled, not merely because of a background of hostile traditions, but also because of the contemporary forces which sustained that background, in logical conformity with current needs. Thus the dominant political philosophy of the modern Japanese business class was an organic theory of state. It was this concept which showed through in its theory of representation, one that continued to center in the idea of the integration of parties, bureaucracy, and Emperor. Here was not only a theory which encouraged irresponsibility, but one which could never remove Japanese politics far from the shadow of authoritarianism. The organic premise also colored any appreciation of individual dignity and rights, establishing as it did a primacy of state power and authority. At the same time, it contributed to the expression of personal interests through subterranean channels, symbolizing the lack of a philosophy which would give adequate ethical support to the open expression of individual or group interests. In the absence of a theory which would recognize the legitimacy of private interests, there was a compulsion on the part of the business class to protect and advance its interests secretly, with minimal resort to open political action or democratic procedures. This in turn tended to produce in the class as a whole a schizophrenic approach to the very concept of democracy, and on occasion a personal guilt complex which later helped to create many cases of recantation of Westernism. In some individuals the conflict was very intense, with all the overtones of tragedy and pathos.

A more detailed explanation of the forces that caused this philosophic dilemma, with particular emphasis on their mature forms, is necessary. Of greatest importance was the evolution of Japanese capitalism. Even when capitalism in Japan reached the stage of its greatest power before World War II and seemed to have captured the commanding heights of Japanese society, it continued to suffer from a sense of great insecurity, and one derivative in part from logical economic grounds. With the extraordinary expansion of industry there loomed up the haunting specter of an artificiality incapable of being sustained by the nature of the domestic market or "normal" foreign trade conditions. In considerable measure Japanese production had been the creature of state necessities or state-projected goals, and in the very rapidity and nature of its growth it tended to be divorced from the assimilative capacities of its society.

The wedding of state power and Western technology had not only drastically affected the structural forms of Japanese capitalism, but had also fashioned a productive machine that could easily run rampant in a society in which conditions suitable for bringing the domestic consumption market into line with productive capacities did not exist. Given the extreme political unbalance in Japanese society itself, there was no forceful pressure to readjust serious economic inequities and broaden the internal market. Moreover, the rising standards, which might in any case have been expected in some degree, were severely restricted by the host of problems connected with population rises out of all proportion to land area. Hence, even in the era of its greatest glory, Japanese business was acutely aware of its fundamental weaknesses, and consequently of its continued dependency, in the broadest sense, on governmental power and policy. That by now it was a vital part of government itself did not change this psychology. To be sure, there were differences in attitude, as between the *nouveaux riches* and the established zaibatsu, for instance. The former were more dependent upon government, and the latter more interdependent with it, and this created some difference in their respective political attitudes and actions. In the final analysis, however, this fact could not be significant, for, given the nature of the threats and pressures, the emphasis had to be on the supremacy and unity of the state.

Thus, in terms of democratic theory, the Japanese business groups could neither follow the historic Western route of laissez faire nor hew out a different pathway suitable to the circumstances of twentieth-century Japanese society. The latter procedure would have required a more delicate balance of competing forces than was existent in modern Japan; in the very ingredients of overwhelming success lay the materials which precluded the business community from groping its way to the "open society." . . .

Thus the specific emphases of the political activity of businessmen during this period were placed on promoting "probusiness" policies, on resisting agrarian and military elements when their own position seemed threatened, and on opposing any broad social change or reform. In connection with the second emphasis, however, it should be noted that compromise or actual union was not uncommon, the product variously of fear, indecision, or choice. In no case did these policies, however natural, necessarily advance the frontiers of Japanese democracy; many retarded it. And in addition to this expanded role in the active political theater, all the backstage maneuvering characteristic of Japanese political behavior continued, and the flow of money to parties, individual politicians, and public officials became staggering in its volume and scope. Thus the years of "party government" produced in the public mind a picture of callous disregard for the needs of the lower classes and of a continuous series of scandals dwarfing the prior disclosures of corruption, without successfully establishing the major philosophic premises of democracy. . . .

The concentration of financial and industrial controls was greatly speeded up after 1920, spurred on by general economic conditions and government policy. . . .

. . . Democracy and the party system were now equated by many with political corruption, domination by vested interests, selfishness, and depression. As their strength ebbed away, the parties were powerless to withstand attack from without and disintegration from within.

It has been our purpose . . . to indicate the role that Japanese capitalism played in this unfolding tragedy, and in so doing, to lay out one very fundamental problem which Japanese democracy faced and to which no solution was found. The Japanese industrial revolution was borne on the wings of state power, making use of modern techniques developed and advanced by the West. That this was a most natural — indeed, indispensable — development was implicit in the whole timing of that revolution in relation to the Japanese past and the Western present. Herein a central problem of Japanese democracy was posed. Western democracy had followed a leisurely evolutionary development strongly shaped in the early modern period by the economic and political interests of the middle class. If the Western liberal societies experienced an initial period of mercantilism and extensive commercial dependency upon state power, important changes subsequently occurred. The increasing power of the business community made possible and demanded a transition to modified laissez faire. In part this increased business power was the product of the natural advantages of the society, such as resources, location, and labor supply; in major degree, it was the result of a head start in the process of political and commercial-industrial modernization. . . . Consequently, a relatively great degree of competition could prevail under modified laissez faire (in the beginning stages at least), precluding rapid concentrations, broadening the base of commercial-industrial groups, and making the term "middle class" meaningful. And in the transition and the period which followed, the middle class expressed its philosophy in the concepts of limitations upon the power of government, representative supremacy in government, and individual dignity and rights. If in expressing these ideas it was voicing selected passages from the whole literature of Western political tradition, still their force and vitality came from the fact that they represented the living realities of immediate interest. Armed with this philosophy and the concessions won on behalf of it, the business community assumed an increasingly important position in shaping the institutions which governed the whole of its society. Moreover, the progress of industrialization over the decades, though not without its corrosive influences, gradually made the democratic creed meaningful to the lower economic classes and gave them the power to effectuate some of the premises of that creed. Then the state took on the role of adjuster of conflicting interests more or less adequately represented in the power balance.

In modern Japan, however, it was not possible to duplicate this historic process, nor to find, at least in the prewar period, a satisfactory substitute for it which would help to make democratic principles meaningful to the society, and effective. The modern Japanese business class was the product of much more than a set of traditions adverse to its acceptance of Western-style democracy; it was the result of a timing sequence which sustained many of these traditions and projected them in modern form. . . . Even if the Japanese resource-population balance had been more favorable, or less aggravated by the impact of capitalism, there would have remained in some degree the continued pressure of the advanced industrial West, and one composed of such a myriad of advantages as to be not easily overcome. But even if this had been possible — and one cannot deny that in the 1930's it loomed as a possibility — there remained the supreme fact that the neomercantilist pattern of development, armed with the end product of Western technological evolution, would have already shaped the commercial-industrial structure to such a degree and in such a manner as to make its economic and political forms extremely difficult to remold, barring internal or external violence.

It was within these forms that the Japanese business class existed and developed its political creed and action. Out of its own structure, its relation to government, and its needs, came an organic theory of politics and society. The paternalism which was a part of Japanese tradition was revitalized in the public relations between business and government, and hence sustained in the private relations between employer and employee, businessman and official. Moreover, the concurrent development of nationalism and industrialization caused primary stress to be placed upon the responsibility of capitalism to the state, with its obligations to the individual considered a matter of secondary importance. The emphases on power over freedom, on the state over the individual, and on unity over a true recognition and representation of conflicting interests — all were derivatives from the central premises. That these — premises and derivatives alike — formed the underpinning for the political action of the prewar business community as a whole is demonstrated by the history of that action. Their activity on behalf of a completely inte-

grated political force was perhaps the most revealing example.

To state these generalizations so baldly is of course to pay less attention than is necessary to developmental changes in the economic, social, and political position of commerce and the business class; but when one has uncovered and analyzed these, the generalizations can still be left basically unchanged. It is also true that in positing these conclusions, insufficient justice is being meted out to the individual exceptions and to the general conflict within almost all elements of the business community. That there were some who desired it otherwise, some whose ideals and philosophy rested solidly with those of Western democracy, is readily admitted; it is even more important to acknowledge the fact that varying degrees of ambivalence, contradiction, and tension were a very real part of the over-all political position of the business classes. Indeed, tension and conflict were present throughout the whole of modern Japanese society, despite the institutions and goals, or perhaps because of them. One does not need to deny any of this nor try to draw the lines of morality and immorality, however, in order to establish the dominant traits of business politics, its causes, and its results.

One final aspect of the problem is to be noted. Japanese capitalism entered the world scene at a time when classical liberalism was close to its zenith and was producing its own social and economic problems. It was already under growing attack in the countries of its origins. Only in those Western nations which under the old system had enjoyed a maximum of advantages and a minimum of social ills, only in those whose traditions now rested firmly upon political liberalism, was there a certain resiliency to the revolutionary currents of the extreme left and right. This resiliency enabled certain nations to undertake experiments with new forms of mixed economies which would permit the retention of basic democratic values, experiments that are still proceeding. In Japan, capitalism created great social and economic problems, without building any solid liberal foundations in its society. It could produce neither spectacular improvements in mass living standards nor a dynamic, new political philosophy. Consequently, it operated under the threat of a revolutionary attack, with few of the circumstances present which would encourage democratic tactics or moderation. In its failures as well as in its strengths, Japanese capitalism was of too little service to the democratic cause.

Movements to Protect Constitutional Government — A Structural-Functional Analysis

ISHIDA TAKESHI

We come now to a political explanation as to why the forces that opposed the power structure were unable to change it sufficiently to institute "party rule" as a permanent aspect of government in prewar Japan. The author, Dr. Ishida, is an assistant professor of political science at Tōkyō University where he studied.

The structural-functional method which he uses here is one which attempts to probe the real power structure and then determine what role or function the political parties and other elements played in its operation. To determine the function of various groups, Dr. Ishida examines their objectives. For instance, he notes that the parties wanted more power than they had, so they attacked the positions of strength of the ruling elite, but in order to be effective, they had to mobilize popular opinion on their side. They appealed to the people with promises of lower taxes or universal suffrage. Thus, they played a democratic role. But simultaneously they also played an authoritarian role inasmuch as they rallied the electorate to support the "emperor system" in which the Diet was relatively unimportant.

When the parties did push through manhood suffrage, it was hedged in by an anti-subversive law and in other ways so that it did not constitute a strong democratic advance. The parties were able simply to extend their established lines of influence, especially in the countryside. In fighting among themselves, they subsequently appealed to anti-democratic sentiments and ideas, which tended to undermine the party system itself. The proletarian parties did not become as great a threat to them as expected, for they were not only legally circumscribed but the social structure of their support was still weak. As a result, this analysis is very pessimistic about prewar democratic potentials.

THE STRUCTURE OF "PARTY RULE" IN PREWAR JAPAN

The first question we shall deal with is why "party government" or "party rule" (*seitō seiji*) under the name of "the normal path of constitutional government" (*kensei no jōdō*) became such an important political objective in the period known as "Taishō democracy" (*Taishō demokurashī*). . . .

From Ishida Takeshi, *Kindai Nihon Seiji Kōzō no Kenkyū* (*A Study of the Political Structure of Modern Japan*) (Tōkyō: Mirai-sha, 1956), pp. 131–250, translated and summarized by George O. Totten with permission of the author and the Mirai-sha.

As this becomes clearer in terms of an analysis of the Japanese political "structure" at the time, the next related question that will be taken up is why "party government" had to meet the fate of a gradual "decline" in the first few years of the Shōwa period which began in 1926.

These two questions will be discussed primarily by analyzing the "structure" of "party government" in prewar Japan. In the first section below, the initial question will be clarified in the light of the historically antecedent "constitutional government protection" campaign of 1912–13. The second section will then continue the discussion through 1925 when "universal suffrage" became the burning issue raised by the three-party coalition of the second "constitutional government protection" campaign. In the third section, the question of the "decline of party government" will be studied, asking why it was necessary that the bureaucracy (including the military) should emerge dominant. Although these sections roughly correspond to chronological events, our main concern here is not with recounting history but with defining the characteristics of the political structure in each phase in order to determine what similarities run through them and what changes have taken place. The changes in the social structure that gave rise to these campaigns will be analyzed and the way they in turn affected the political process will be indicated.

THE FIRST CAMPAIGN FOR THE PROTECTION
OF CONSTITUTIONAL GOVERNMENT
(1912–16)

Some historians date the history of political parties in Japan from 1874 when the agitation for the establishment of a popularly elected assembly began. Others see parties as first becoming important at the time of the first Ōkuma-Itagaki "party cabinet" of 1898, followed by Itō Hirobumi's decision to organize the Seiyūkai, the party that was to last till 1940. But there are reasons why I consider the campaign of 1912–13 to "overthrow the oligarchy and pro-

tect constitutional government," as the period with which to begin a study of "party government" in pre-World War II Japan. . . .

This campaign grew up around the demand that the political parties, still weak in relation to the ruling oligarchy, actually assume a major role in government. Of course, this was a demand that had grown only gradually. This did not mean simply that the Japanese bourgeoisie demanded power and wanted to rule through political parties, as was the case in modern France. The Japanese industrial and landlord classes had other sources and means of power. But it did mean that, within the tight confines of the Meiji constitution and its extra-constitutional framework, the forces from below, including the "fourth estate," were demanding greater say in government and that changes were taking place within the so-called "emperor system" (tennōsei taisei) that were making this appear possible. . . .

Another reason for dating the trend toward "party government" from this period is that for the first time the phrase "protect constitutional government" became to a degree a popular slogan. It was hurled against the third Katsura (December 1912 to February 1913) and the first Yamamoto cabinets (February 1913 to April 1914) and proved to be a highly effective weapon in interparty struggle. . . .

This slogan also proved to be most effective in mobilizing and focusing popular support from below. If we compare this campaign with the mass demonstrations at the time of the signing of the Russo-Japanese peace treaty in September 1905, this fact becomes clear. At that time when riots broke out, attacks were made against progovernment newspapers and police boxes were destroyed. Though originally incited by the "hard-line" political leaders who opposed compromising the gains of victory in the war, the riots went far beyond anything they anticipated and the mobs soon got out of hand.

Similar riots broke out in the "constitution-protection" campaign of 1912–13. This time, however, popular sentiment was stirred up by politicians who were able to manipulate it to a far greater extent than in the riots against the Russo-Japanese peace treaty. To be sure, the campaign was not completely controlled by the parties, because some of the politicians who championed the constitutional government cause, such as Inukai Tsuyoshi and Ozaki Yukio, were not under the thumb of top party discipline. They often acted on their own initiative. But they were able to give the campaign the cast of a movement of the people against oligarchic and bureaucratic government, despite its actually being led by various small groups. It gained vitality from being linked up with other issues that affected large numbers of the populace, such as opposition to certain taxes. In any case, it was a characteristic of the 1912–13 and subsequent campaigns against the Ōkuma Cabinet (April 1914 to October 1916) that they differed from the 1905 riots in supporting the political parties "from below" and in helping to bring about cabinet changes. . . .

"Protecting constitutional government" meant different things to different groups and classes of people. To the political party leaders, it connoted certain reforms to help them in their struggle against the clan oligarchy, as represented by the Elder Statesmen or Genrō, and the bureaucracy, including the military with its special privileges. To the business community, it held up the goal of "cheap government," inasmuch as reductions in expenditures for the bureaucracy and the military could more easily be effected if the Diet played a larger role in approving the budget. To the populace at large, it had the emotive meaning of generally more representative, less arbitrary rule.

More specifically, the political leaders saw this slogan as an attack on the arbitrary utilization by the Genrō and others in the clan oligarchy of "commands" from the throne to overcome opposition to measures they desired. The passing of the charismatic

Meiji Emperor in 1912 raised the question as to who was really responsible for the Emperor's words in such cases. The answer was clearly still the Genrō. But the Elder Statesmen that most readily came to mind at that time were Yamagata Aritomo and his protégé Katsura Tarō, who were widely disliked if not hated by the articulate populace. As they and the other Elder Statesmen began to work more and more through the Privy Council and the House of Peers, these institutions, too, came under attack. Their reform was called for rather persistently in the early 1920's. In 1912–13, however, it was still too early for that. The House of Peers was easily able to bring down the Yamamoto Cabinet in 1914. Ōkuma became Premier next with a secret understanding with the Genrō that the army would get the two new divisions it had been demanding. Nevertheless, times had changed, for Ozaki, who in 1898 had suffered from criticism of his speech in which he conjectured about conditions in Japan "if it were a republic," was able without being again accused of "lese majesty" to castigate Katsura in 1913 for using an imperial edict for his own purposes. . . .

Another aspect of "constitutional government," as far as the politicians were concerned, was the regaining for the cabinet of the right to appoint certain civil servants and cabinet ministers without restrictions. That would mean squashing the two main prevailing restrictions. One was that, since 1894, requirements for office-holding had been such as to effectively keep politicians out of the civil service. The other required, since 1900, that only generals (and lieutenant generals) and admirals (and vice-admirals) on the active list could be appointed War or Navy Minister respectively. This actually gave the military great power over the life of a cabinet, since, if an appointment that displeased the high command was made, the appointee could be immediately retired and thus become ineligible for office. This could cause the cabinet to fall. It was General Yamagata, "father" of both the army and the civil service, who pushed through these regulations with an eye to crippling the power of the political parties.

For this reason, the slogan for "overthrowing the oligarchy" (*batsuzoku daha*) constituted an attack against the bureaucracy. The politicians hoped to open the civil service to a kind of spoils system. This they partly succeeded in doing during the Yamamoto Cabinet in 1913. At the same time they gained the important concession which allowed reserve generals and admirals, as well as those on the active list, to be eligible for the posts of War and Navy Minister. (This modification was again wiped out in 1936 under the Hirota Cabinet.) . . .

The outcry against the restrictions on the cabinet in making War Ministry appointments reached a crescendo in December 1912 when it became the immediate cause for the downfall of the Saionji Cabinet. By refusing to recommend a successor to the War Minister who had just resigned, the military forced Saionji to submit his own resignation. War Minister Uehara had insisted on the creation of two additional army divisions even in the face of the passage by both houses of the appropriations bill which embodied a policy of retrenchment. It was, of course, Prince Yamagata who was behind the demand for the army divisions, but he may also have just used this issue as a weapon to pull down the cabinet for the larger purpose of pursuing a stronger policy toward China. What he and others of the Chōshū and Satsuma clan oligarchs feared especially was the subversive influence of "republican" ideas from China which were spreading with the outbreak of the Chinese Revolution of 1911. The two division increase at this time was not an expression of the growing independence of the military in Japanese political life as was the case in the 1930's. Rather, it reflected the fear of the still rather integrated group of Elder Statesmen, and the older ruling forces on which they rested, that a disintegration was

setting in in the very structure of their power. They assessed the political parties to be one of the new, albeit still despicable, forces for change.

Political parties had grown considerably in influence from the late 1890's. The alliance of Itō Hirobumi with the Jiyūtō (Liberal Party) and Matsukata with the Kaishintō (Reform Party) brought party and clan bureaucrats together. This was furthered by Itō's decision to organize the Seiyūkai (Political Friends Party) in 1900. Even Yamagata followed suit, asking Ōura to organize the parliamentary party called the Chūō Kurabu (Central Club). In 1912 Katsura recognized the necessity of forming a national (and nationalistic) party. But one should be careful to understand that this rise in party influence did not come about necessarily at the expense of bureaucratic power. By and large the politicians and the bureaucrats promoted their mutual interests. However, when, also during the Yamamoto Cabinet, the politicians cut down the bureaucracy by 6,428 posts and reduced its budget by ¥4,000,000, this was an expression of the larger forces *behind* the politicians' demand for "cheaper government." . . .

This last point, as earlier mentioned, constituted another element in the meaning of the slogan for the "protection of constitutional government." Both this administrative reform and the opposition to the additional two divisions would help achieve government retrenchment. This would help make possible a tax reduction. In 1912 the government had promised to reduce income and business taxes, but this promise was sacrificed for military expansion. Immediately, widespread agitation for tax reduction developed. A noteworthy instance was a mass meeting in Tōkyō on January 20, 1914, which soon inspired rallies in Ōsaka, Kyōto, Nagoya, and elsewhere, demanding that the government economize through administrative and financial measures and through desisting from undertaking any new non-emergency projects. The Siemens affair of bribery in naval contracts added fuel to the fire. Typically, however, the nationwide movement became blunted by factional quarrels among the leaders and by being sidetracked into an anti-China policy. It was, of course, actually killed by the response of "national unity" to the outbreak of the World War in 1914.

The "constitutional government" slogan had gained popular support by being identified with the demand for the "overthrow the clan oligarchy," and at the same time it provided the politicians with a substantive program in the eyes of the taxpayers who, especially since the end of the Meiji period in 1912, were becoming increasingly conscious of their role as a source of money and therefore as a source of power through the politicians. . . .

The greater popularity of political campaigns and the consequent increase in party strength are confirmed by detailed studies of the period which show that business organizations had become more interested than ever in elections. There was an increase in the number of Diet members who were of business background, though by and large business preferred to work through professional party leaders. The main political interest the various business groups had in common at this time was the desire for lowered taxes and the consequent reduction in what was labeled "unproductive" military spending. . . .

Slogans attacking the oligarchy and calling for constitutional government could canalize the widespread discontent of those strata of the urban populace that had sufficient income to qualify them as voters under the restricted suffrage. Their votes were mobilized by local bosses of various kinds. But the more intense discontent of the mass of workers and the small farmers and tenant farmers was not mobilized for political purposes. Nevertheless, even this degree of political mobilization and canalization brought about a weakening of the old power structure. The most violent party-haters, Yamagata and Katsura, were forced to reckon with the activities of the

political parties. They had to fight fire with fire and had to broaden their own influence among those forces which constituted their natural opposition. Katsura, for instance, brought into his Rikken Dōshikai (Constitutional Comrades Party) rather important figures from the financial world. As a result, when this party attacked the Yamamoto Cabinet in the name of "constitutional government," it was not a simple conflict between the bureaucrats and business (since Katsura was a bureaucrat and yet many of his supporters were from the business community) nor was it just a fight between the clan oligarchy and the political parties (for the clan oligarchy included Yamagata and his protégé Katsura and at the same time Katsura and his supporters were organized in the Rikken Dōshikai, which was a political party of sorts). The opponents were overlapping to a degree. So it was obviously more complicated than that; but still that was it in outline.

In conclusion, we can say that the forces opposing the power structure had not yet built their own political leadership, but they were infiltrating and confusing the old structure, causing a degree of readjustment, although their own independent power was being somewhat neutralized in the process. The process, nevertheless, had reached such a point by the time the oligarchy reluctantly decided to recommend Hara Satoshi, the first "commoner," to the premiership in 1918 that this decision can be considered a turning point on the road to "constitutional government." . . .

THE SECOND CAMPAIGN FOR THE PROTECTION OF CONSTITUTIONAL GOVERNMENT AND THE ENACTMENT OF UNIVERSAL SUFFRAGE (1923–25)

Roughly ten years lapsed between the beginning of the first and the beginning of the second movement to protect constitutional government. But despite the similarity in name, the second movement developed within a far more favorable context, one which witnessed the enactment of universal manhood suffrage in 1925, To be sure, agitation for universal suffrage dated from the turn of the century, but the whole question of greater popular participation gained a new dimension with the outbreak of the rice riots of 1918 sufficient to enable one to say that a new phase had been reached in the long struggle for popularly responsible, constitutional government. . . .

The new atmosphere is suggested by the comment of a contemporary editorial written in reference to the Siberian expedition which was almost simultaneously begun in the early days of August 1918. The Ōsaka *Asahi* commented on the 22nd that, due to the rice riots, the reaction of the people to the dispatch of troops to Siberia differed from that to all previous events which involved Japan militarily. The people had previously always promptly forgotten their own grievances and in effect asked the government in what way they could help in the war effort. But now for the first time their reaction was only a more insistent demand as to what the government could do to relieve their own plight.

Truly the rice riots constituted the first popular movement that had sprung up spontaneously without party or other leadership and did so on a national scale. This was frightening to the ruling groups including the party leaders. They thus began to take more seriously various popular demands, including that for the suffrage, for fear that the people would otherwise express themselves in extra-political terms. In this sense, a new phase in the struggle for popular rights had begun.

The rice riots shook the country as a whole, although they lacked the focus for independent political action. The appointment of Hara to the premiership, since he was not only the first "commoner" to be so honored but also because he was the first real party boss, constituted a concession by the Elder Statesmen in the face of the popular discontent the people were evincing concerning conditions for which the Genrō were ultimately responsible. Although this discontent was not great

enough to cause a change in the structure of their rule, it was clear to them that conditions had matured to the point where independent political action could be taken by the masses and in this sense, too, a new phase had been reached. . . .[1]

In this new phase in the development toward responsible government, the demand for "universal suffrage" joined the earlier slogans of "Establish party cabinet!" and "End the rule of special privilege!" as part of the new meaning of the term "constitutional government."

More specifically the three-party coalition was based upon two principles enunciated on January 17, 1924: "(1) We shall coordinate our actions in future for the purpose of protecting constitutional government and establishing parliamentary rule. (2) Our immediate objective is to oppose and overthrow the Kiyoura special-privilege cabinet and set up a party cabinet." . . .

The concrete meaning of "party cabinet," however, was nowhere spelled out. As in the earlier movement, the negative aspect of opposition to the encumbent cabinet was foremost. But in both cases, the parties also had positive aims. In the earlier movement, the way they proposed to effectuate the "overthrow of the oligarchy" was to change the Civil Service Appointments Ordinance. And the way the second movement hoped to "end special privilege" was to reform the House of Peers. But for these aims to be realized, the parties in both periods needed popular support. The slo-

---

[1] In a footnote, Mr. Ishida explains that Yamagata agreed to Hara's cabinet because he thought that if the parties' demands for a party government were disappointed at that moment, they would form a united front and really push for the institution of "party rule" as a regular thing, but if the Genrō acceded to party government by Hara now, it would eventually meet such trouble that supra-party cabinets could again be formed. This meant that "the first real party cabinet" was approved by Yamagata on the grounds that it would prevent subsequent party coalitions for the purpose of forming party government. Mr. Ishida refers for his materials on this point to Hara Satoshi, *Nikki*, Vol. 5, pp. 28–29 and *passim*. [Editor's note]

gan they adopted for that purpose in the first instance was the reduction of taxes. In the second case, it was the demand for universal suffrage.

In the demand for reform of the House of Peers — and much more so with regard to universal suffrage — the newspapers were ahead of the parties. But the reform even they called for was very mild; it consisted of three limitations: (1) on the number of members of the House of Peers by inheritance, (2) on the number of imperial appointees for life, and (3) on the length of time the Peers could deliberate on the budget.

The two main reasons for the mildness of the demands were, of course, one, the virtual impossibility of amending the Meiji Constitution and, two, the weakness of the popular bases of the political parties. The liberal professor Yoshino Sakuzō argued that the only way for the lower house to prevail against the upper was to have the lower house gain the moral superiority of truly representing the vast majority of the people. The idea of representation took various forms but most rested on the contention that under the impact of capitalist development the class structure had changed, rendering the Meiji dispensation obsolescent. Proposals for more clearly articulated functional, class, or occupational representation in both houses were circulated. But by and large the political parties were mainly interested in preventing the repetition of supra-party cabinets based on the House of Peers. . . .

The demand for universal suffrage was much more important because it would produce a greater change in the operation of the political process and because it had a far greater appeal to the public than reform of the House of Peers and as such could affect the very nature of the parties themselves. Though this demand had been to an extent articulated since the middle of the Meiji period and even became a proposed bill in the Diet of 1902, the subsequent development of the mass media, especially the newspapers, and the spread of discontent among the articulate intelligentsia created new conditions for its drawing support from the masses. This time it differed from all previous political demands in that it was not created by the parties simply to canalize popular support for their own ends but actually propelled the parties to take some concrete action — which in fact they eventually did. . . .

In any review of the role of party leaders with regard to universal suffrage, it must be pointed out that Hara was sincerely opposed to such an extension of the franchise, thinking it would "ruin the country," as he confided to his diary. And as he warned in his statement on dissolving the Diet on February 26, 1920, he felt the suffrage bill was "hastily and lightly" conceived and did not accord with the conditions of the country and that it "harbored disturbing ideas that threatened the existing social structure." The fact is that Hara wished to introduce a system of small electoral districts and reorganize his party before experimenting with extending the suffrage. . . .

In contrast to Hara, how was Katō Takaaki, the leader of the rival Kenseikai party, reacting to the suffrage issue? It is clear that at first (even in March 1921), Katō himself did not favor universal suffrage. But, pressed by his own supporters and in order to take issue with the Seiyūkai, Katō came out publicly in favor of it. His rationalization was that the "public will" should be guided, not suppressed, and that the interests of the various classes in society should be harmonized and not be made to clash. Representation for the majority of the people within the Diet was the best way to assure class harmony, he averred. . . .

Now what about the Seiyūkai, which, under Hara, had buried the suffrage bill in 1920? How did it come around to becoming one of the three parties in the coalition that passed manhood suffrage in 1925? We are still considering just the top leadership. After Hara's assassination, Takahashi Korekiyo became head of the party and Prime Minister (November 1921 to June 1922) but was unable to maintain himself in power long, because of strife within the Seiyūkai. When he fell, the logical man to recommend, from the point of view of responsible constitutional government, would have been Katō Takaaki, but this Takahashi feared. Instead, he forcefully recommended Admiral Katō Tomosaburō who promptly formed a supra-party cabinet, despite the offer of unconditional support by the Seiyūkai. Still, this cabinet lasted only till August 1923 when the Admiral died. It was followed by Admiral Yamamoto's cabinet which, however, resigned before the year was out. Still the Genrō feared Katō Takaaki and instead chose Count Kiyoura Keigo, a member of the House of Peers, who formed a cabinet in January 1924 from members of the Kenkyūkai (Study Society) group in the House of Peers. A few of the leaders of the Seiyūkai split off, calling themselves the Seiyūhontō (Real Political Friends Party) and supported Kiyoura as a government party. But to say that the Seiyūkai changed its position on the suffrage question because of their defection is to overlook the opinion on the matter held by Takahashi, the leader of the Seiyūkai. . . .

Takahashi's position was actually about the same as that of Katō Takaaki, namely, that, if the suffrage were not granted, the political demand for it would turn into a socialist movement, which if further frustrated could become a revolutionary force. He felt that the political acumen of the people was still not yet sufficiently matured, but nevertheless, under the circumstances, it would be better to extend the suffrage early and thus prevent the growth of more radical ideas later.

The party leaders, Katō of the Kenseikai, Takahashi of the Seiyūkai, and Inukai of the Kakushin (Reform) Club joined together to oppose the "non-party" Kiyoura Cabinet. They were fundamentally agreed that they did not want the present "political" demands to turn into "social" demands in the future (that is, into demands for changes in the social structure). But their immediate interests were in overthrowing the Kiyoura Cabinet and in setting up their coalition. They called for checking the power of the groups of special privilege, such as the Kenkyūkai of the House of Peers, and establishing a party cabinet but said nothing about the suffrage. It was their dilemma to want to overthrow the Kiyoura Cabinet and yet not be able to gain the popular support to do so without taking up the suffrage issue. It was only really when they realized that the suffrage issue was not only popular but was actively being supported by organized groups that they seriously took cognizance of it.

Only after the three-party coalition was consummated did the demand for universal suffrage reach full flower as a political party issue. It was characterized by three features, unprecedented by suffrage campaigns prior to the rice riots of 1918. First, by 1919 it had become a mass movement. Secondly, it had assumed more than a temporary focus by the participation of labor unions. And thirdly, under such slogans as "the worker-student front" (*rōgaku teikei*), the students, as differentiated from the wider intelligentsia, began to play a part in it.

How different from the first campaign for universal suffrage was the sight of ranks of workers, students, and city people (*shimin*) marching in step to the tune of the "Universal Suffrage Song"!

All this talk about "labor" being "sacred!"
  Yoi, yoi,
  Why don't they give us the right to vote?
  Yōi, yōi, democracy!
Who harvests the rice? Who tills the fields?
  Yoi, yoi,
  Why don't they give us the right to vote?
  Yōi, yōi, democracy!
Shouldn't everything be governed by public
  opinion? *Yoi, yoi,*
  Why don't they give us the right to vote?
  Yōi, yōi, democracy!
Only by our digging coal can the machines
  run. *Yoi, yoi,*

Why don't they give us the right to vote?
　Yōi, yōi, democracy!
We launched the war ships. *Yoi, yoi,*
　Why don't they give us the right to vote?
　Yōi, yōi, democracy!
They give it to the playboy sons of the rich.
　Yoi, yoi,
　Why don't they give us the right to vote?
　Yōi, yōi, democracy!
[As soldiers,] our regimental flags are soaked
　in blood. *Yoi, yoi,*
　Why don't they give us the right to vote?
　Yōi, yōi, democracy!

The number of labor unions had grown from forty in 1917 to three hundred in 1922. In the background the Russian revolution had heightened the workers' consciousness of their own legal rights and their need for autonomous action. The organized workers and their leaders were becoming increasingly aware of the need for universal suffrage as a means for opposing legislative action they considered detrimental to their real rights. For example, the Yūaikai (Friendly Society — the main union federation at the time) at its emergency general meeting of March 10, 1919 linked up the demand for universal suffrage with the specific resolution to oppose the legal obstacle to union organization (Article 17 of the Peace Police Law). Many signature petitions were circulated to support this, and Representative Imai Kakō, known as the "patron saint" of universal suffrage, presented in the Diet the signed petition for revision of the Peace Police Law. . . .

But labor support was by no means given in a steadily increasing volume. The fervor of organized labor for the right to vote rose and fell. In 1919 when the suffrage was first blocked by Hara, eighteen of the most important labor unions formed an organization to fight for the suffrage. In the following year large campaigns among organized labor were mounted in both the Kantō and Kansai areas around speech meetings and street demonstrations; labor delegations visited the headquarters of each of the political parties; and unions sent resolutions to the newspapers. In the elections of May 10, 1920, following Hara's dissolution of the Diet on the suffrage issue, all of the representatives, except those from Tōkyō, who favored universal suffrage, lost, including Imai Kakō, while the Seiyūkai gained almost a three-fifths majority. The consequent disillusionment of labor with the parties and the parliamentary process was great, and this opened the way for the rise of anarcho-syndicalism for a time in the ranks of labor. Organized agitation for the suffrage subsided and criticism from labor was directed against the "professional politicians." For instance, in the August 1919 convention of the Sōdōmei (General Federation of Labor — the new name for the Yūaikai) the demand for the suffrage was adopted; in 1920 it became a central demand; in 1921 the Kantō federations asked that the demand be dropped and be replaced by a call for a (syndicalist) general strike, but this was defeated by opposition from the Kansai federations; in 1922 the suffrage demand was dropped. . . .

The change of policy in organized labor was not the only reason for the decline in mass support for the suffrage. The lack of political clarity of purpose and the infiltration of opportunistic elements into the movement were complicating factors. For instance, on February 11, 1920, the groups that met to demand the suffrage included not only bona fide labor unions but also right-wing groups such as labor gangs under the control of local bosses who often acted as a kind of lobbyist group (*ingaidan*) pressuring members of the Diet. At another meeting the same year, along with the demand for the suffrage, the cabinet was attacked for being too soft in its foreign policy, which muddied the issue. This kind of thing dampened the ardor of organized labor for the suffrage but at the same time increased the appetite of the main political parties for control of the sentiment. There is evidence that the *ingaidan* rather than being used by the parties against each other, as was usually the case, actually brought to the attention of the party leadership (of the Kenseikai especially) the popularity of the sentiment in favor of the suffrage. . . .

A new development in the second movement for constitutional government was the important role played by students. Students were a significant proportion of the some 1,800 people who were arrested by the police, if not long detained, during this movement at various times. Shortly after the rice riots, students at such universities as Tōkyō, Meiji, Keiō, Nihon, and Waseda in Tōkyō and several in Kyōto organized "Student Worker Clubs" (Rōgakkai), one of whose main demands was for universal suffrage. The joint meeting they held at Hibiya Park on February 11, 1919, the thirtieth anniversary of the Constitution, was unquestionably one of the peaks of the earlier phase of this second movement. In the following year some of them were injured in clashes with the police. But the students were influenced by the same forces as organized labor and paralleled their temporary turn away from parliamentarism. This is not to deny that there was a minor current of the student movement which did use the suffrage issue during this period as a bridge toward getting into politics (especially with the Kenseikai and Kokumintō) as professional politicians or lobbyists (ingaidan), but by 1923 the main current of the student movement preferred working directly with labor and the tenant farmers. While they favored universal suffrage, they did not want to be "used" by the political parties for the latter's own ends, and therefore, they continued their own independent organizations rather than merging their identity into a mass movement on this issue. Organized labor, the tenant farmers associations, and the students federations acted in concert, while maintaining their distance from the established parties during the denouement of the movement to gain the suffrage in 1923–25. . . .

Finally, it should be noted that the newspapers played an important role in both recruiting and moderating popular opinion through their editorials and the other writings of the journalists (who are classified by the Japanese as intellectuals). Already around 1922–23 most of the newspapers supported universal suffrage and attacked the government on this issue. This was true to a certain extent during the first constitutional government movement, but at that time several papers opposed it and favored the Katsura government. Two of the latter became the objects of violence. By the time of the second movement, however, no newspapers were strictly identified as "pro-government." They had come to reflect public opinion to a greater extent and they were becoming more truly mass media. On the other hand, their opinions were modified by the fact that they were becoming part of big business. In the almost two decades since the Russo-Japanese War the capital of the *Asahi* had grown ten times, and the *Mainichi* twenty times. Thus, while they expressed a certain amount of radicalism behind the veil of objectively reporting the "popular will," the newspaper journalists as employees of the big dailies were more circumscribed in their agitation than that small section of the intellectuals who threw their lot in with the labor movement. . . .

THE "NORMAL PATH OF CONSTITUTIONAL GOVERNMENT" AND THE "UNDERMINING OF PARTY RULE" (1925–32)

The period from the Katō Kenseikai Cabinet (1925–26), following the three-party coalition which passed the suffrage bill, to the Inukai Seiyūkai Cabinet 1931–32) marked what historians often call the period of "party rule" or "party government." More correctly it should be considered the period in which the *possibility* of "the normal path of constitutional government" existed. That phrase, of course, had various meanings in that period of great political strife. It was used as ammunition against cabinets that compromised with anti-parliamentary forces or ruled in the name of "national unity." But it theoretically referred to governments whose prime minister was chosen by the majority party and thus in some way reflected the will of the majority of the voters. It meant a cabinet that was responsible to the Diet and thus ultimately to the electorate. As Professor Yoshino detected, it signified a shift in the point of gravity from the *Genrō* and *Jūshin* (Senior Statesmen) to the political parties, an evolution different from that originally intended by the creators of the Meiji constitutional dispensation. The passage of the universal suffrage bill laid the necessary precondition for its realization. . . .

Despite the existence of this precondition, party rule failed. This consummation was not entirely imposed by extra-parliamentary forces, such as the military and the bureaucracy, but was to a degree brought about by the parties themselves whose words and actions contradicted the concept of party rule. These words and deeds can be discussed in two categories: (1) those touching the question of the "national polity" (*kokutai*) and (2) those having to do with corruption. . . .

Vague and mystical as it was, the "national polity" was not just an abstract concept. For instance, in 1928 during the first national election carried out on the basis of manhood suffrage, the Seiyūkai attacked the Minseitō for including in its platform the idea that the Diet should be the "center" of the political process (*gikai-chūshinshugi*), arguing that such an idea "violated the national polity." And conversely the Minseitō in 1932 insisted that the Inukai Seiyūkai Cabinet was not "carrying out the proper conduct of a subject of the Emperor" in not resigning over the Sakuradamon Affair.[2] It was clear that the concept of the "national polity" could be used to reject the essence of "the normal path of constitutional government." And this both parties did do, not only with their words, but with their actions.

The Seiyūkai lined up with right-wing pressure-lobbyists at the time of the Boku

[2] See glossary. [Editor's note]

Retsu Affair in 1926;[3] after that, the Seiyūkai lined up with the Privy Council, which blocked Premier Wakatsuki's request for an emergency imperial ordinance to save the Bank of Taiwan, bringing down the Wakatsuki cabinet; then there was the understanding among the Seiyūkai, the Privy Council, and the military opposing the London Naval Treaty of 1930 which limited the size of the navy; then even after the end of party cabinets, the Seiyūkai attack the Okada Cabinet (1934–36) for its "organic theory" of the Emperor — all these examples, and many more, can be given to show how the parties by their actions upheld interpretations of the Meiji Constitution that were incompatible with "the normal path of constitutional government."

These actions not only harmed the party in power but cut at the very raison d'être of the parties themselves. They strengthened the non-party forces "above" them (such as the Privy Council). But the parties, through indulging in corruption and then exposing each other's corruption in public, strengthened the anti-party attitudes among the people "below."[4] Unfortunately, these incidents did not just implicate party factions or simply individuals, but came to undermine the confidence of the people in the party system, which was to have been invigorated by universal suffrage, and destroyed their hope for strong, reliable party leadership. The "rotten, corrupt parties" became the target of the budding "fascists.". . .

[3] See glossary. [Editor's note]
[4] Examples: the 1926 incident of the move of the Matsushima gay quarters in Ōsaka; the 1929 incident of the five private railroads involving former Minister of Railways Ogawa Heikichi; the Echigo Railroad incident involving Kobashi Ichita, Minister of Education in the Hamaguchi Minseitō government in November 1929; the incident of selling decorations; the incident of Yamanashi, the Governor General of Korea; and especially in 1929 the Hamaguchi Cabinet with its slogan of "cleaning up the government" exposed the corruption of the Seiyūkai hoping to use this to help it win the elections, but as the decorations-selling incident and the five private railroad incidents came to light, it became clear that the Minseitō was involved and its Minister of Education Kobashi had to resign. [Editor's note]

Why did the parties dig their own graves in this way? The general explanation is that the zaibatsu were paying for the increased costs of election campaigns now that universal suffrage was a reality and then using the parties in squabbling among themselves for various advantages. But let us look a little further into the structure of party support. . . .

If the lower house really felt that it rested on the will of the people, it would have enjoyed a moral superiority over the upper house. But this was not the case. Even party cabinets relied too heavily on the high ministers surrounding the Emperor such as the Grand Chamberlain and the Imperial Household Minister, as, for example, at the time of the Manchurian Incident. Then the Inukai Seiyūkai Cabinet under which the Seiyūkai gained the unprecedented number of 304 seats in 1932 actually found that this large number unsettled rather than strengthened the party leadership. This fact helped account for the Seiyūkai, after Inukai's assassination, quietly standing by and witnessing the formation of the supra-party Saitō Cabinet of "national unity." . . .

With the enlarged franchise, the greatest concern of the main parties was to capture the new voters. The party in power used all the governmental facilities at its command, and the party out of power organized watchers to watch over the government campaign watchers — so great was the mutual suspicion! New slogans to appeal to the voters were fashioned, such as those dealing with prosperity or the lack of it. Mass pamphlets were prepared and, for the first time, posters. Yet propaganda remained peripheral to the two real keys to winning elections, namely, the collection and use of funds and the (closely related) cultivation of the constituency (jiban no kakuho). By and large, it is my hypothesis that, although the main parties did begin to direct propaganda to the masses, this was simply a small addition to the utilization of the traditional vertical lines of influence down through the local bosses or notables and

that the extension of the franchise actually brought about no real change in terms of the structure through which the vote was mobilized. Of course, in the cities some new sub-leaders had already come forth in the struggle for the franchise. The Minseitō absorbed most of these along with more of the city vote. (In 1928 about 24% of the Minseitō's Diet members came from city districts compared to 18% for the Seiyūkai). But in the countryside the general political apathy — despite tenant-farmer disputes — was converted into votes for the traditional parties, except that to an extent the tenant-farmer strata did gain representation in assemblies on the local level in the ranks of the main parties and in the small "proletarian" parties. Yet the very sub-leaders who had stepped forth were the ones who later became disillusioned with party politics and supported the "fascistic" bureaucratic reorganization that led to the disappearance of parties. . . .

But before discussing this, let us examine the role of the "proletarian" parties, asking (1) how they acted as parties and (2) to what extent they opened up a new source of strength in the hitherto disfranchised proletarian masses.

First of all, it must be remembered that while the workers and tenant farmers posed a threat of social unrest in the background of the struggle for the suffrage, they were not the ones who carried it through. This was one reason for the weakness of the proletarian parties from the beginning. For instance, the Sōdōmei, which had backed away from the suffrage movement in 1921–22, again took an interest in it in 1923 after the Yamamoto Cabinet had brought up the idea in a platform plank. Of course, the famous article entitled "For a Change in the Direction of the Proletarian Class," written by the socialist theoretician Yamakawa Hitoshi, had appeared in August 1922, urging "realistic" participation in politics; thus, interest in the suffrage was not entirely externally induced. But by and large, labor was not such a propelling force in the whole process from the enlargement of the vote to the creation of the proletarian parties. While the Political Study Society (Seiji Kenkyūkai) of June 1924, made up of intellectuals of diverse ideological persuasions, including labor leaders, was certainly of crucial importance, it nevertheless disintegrated. This was followed in 1925 by the sorry spectacle of the split in the Sōdōmei, when the more radical, pro-Communist leaders formed the Nihon Rōdō Kumiai Hyōgikai (Council of Japanese Labor Unions). The subsequent factional splits in the new proletarian parties sapped their strength. First there was the question of Bolshevism and later the question of war. For the first time labor, farmer, and other mass organizations were able to effectively influence the election of representatives to the Diet, but there was the danger that these representatives would compromise their principles in playing the "bourgeois" parliamentary game. Besides this, the feuds among the proletarian parties were often reflected back into labor disputes to the advantage of management. Of course, the passage of the Peace Preservation Law exacerbated the anxieties that led to these splits. But beyond that, the Japanese "proletariat" was hardly horizontally integrated; it was shot through with many vertical loyalties and layers that made organization difficult, and these were hardly overcome by appealing to "the whole proletarian class." Even the numerous instances of local union and party cooperation did not lead to coordination on the national level. . . .

Leaders for the labor unions and the proletarian parties came mainly from medial social strata, rather than from among the workers themselves, or from the educated (the intelligentsia), especially those who had studied law. But when they once achieved a leadership position they tended to hinder spontaneous, democratic control from below and tried to canalize the discontent with the status quo into political activity controlled by themselves. In fact, they tended to fall into the pattern of utilizing the traditional, vertical lines of po-

litical loyalty but only directing them to support of the proletarian rather than the established, conservative parties. That is why Yoshino Sakuzō warned that the proletarian masses were being used as a stepping stone by the minority interested in politics. . . .

To be sure, changes in the social structure of labor were taking place that rendered more conservative and more authoritarian the mobilization of political energy even by the proletarian leaders. Among them was the reorganization of jobs that accompanied the introduction of foremen training (*shokuchō kyōiku*) and other on-job training designed to raise the technical competence of labor but also to increase the workers' identification with the enterprise where he was employed. (In time the latter became more important.) Also included was the effect on the workers of the military reorganization, especially the law establishing and regulating youth drill and training centers (*seinen kunrenjo*), which would be set up in privately owned factories and shops to be run by retired military officers, school teachers, or army reservist officers and which in addition to drill, taught nationalistic ethics (*shūshin*) and civics (*kōminka*). In the countryside, the government-supported "movement for the revitalization of the agricultural and fishing village economy" (*nōsan gyoson keizai kōsei undō*) attracted many persons from medial social strata and did affect the traditional village order. . . .

Accompanying these changes were reactions on the part of the people affected toward more self-assertive, independent activity, such as instances where the local branches of the Seinendan (the national government-sponsored youth association) opposed the youth drill and training centers. Worker training programs were sometimes set up on the basis of independent worker-student cooperation and even proletarian farmers' schools. In order to counter this kind of autonomous development by labor, the idea of works councils (labor-management consultation committees) were encouraged by management (starting in 1919 by such councils in the National Railroad). Of course, the group most thoroughly opposed to the whole imperial "establishment" was the Japanese Communist Party founded in 1922. But through repeated mass arrests, it was unable to develop on a national scale. In addition, the narrowness of what it might do legally encouraged both opportunism and ultra-leftism. The fear of suffering the fate of the Communists and the fear of being pushed too far by the radicalism of the masses often spelled compromise and weakness on the part of the legal proletarian leaders, only a few of whom had themselves risen from the ranks of labor. . . .

To hypothesize on why the proletarian parties that had not been driven underground or dissolved by the authorities eventually became ultra-nationalistic and supported Japanese-style "fascism," one must remember that inasmuch as the changes we have been discussing neither fundamentally affected the power structure with the Privy Council "above" nor the basic traditional order of the local notables "below," the proletarian parties could only act as an *additional* channel between these two (as in a sense all the parties did). But to the degree that they claimed to represent something different from the established parties and draw to their support the demands and frustrations of the people, they could only lead them in the direction of "fascism," in the direction of renouncing parliamentarism and the "normal path of constitutional government." While there are many explanations for this, we shall confine ourselves to those having to do with changes in the socio-political structure. . . .

The people should have been able to look to the Diet for authoritative, democratic leadership; in actuality they only got big-name authoritarian leadership. They could thus easily become disillusioned with parliamentarism. But this authoritarian leadership had not been provided by "fascist" political parties. Rather it had been supplied by a government which was domi-

nated by the bureaucratic power constellation of the "emperor system." In demanding a "new structure" (*shin taisei*) and in taking a leading part in the formation of the Imperial Rule Assistance Association and the Patriotic Industrial Association (*Sangyō Hōkoku Kai* — modeled after the Nazi *Arbeitsfront*), the proletarian leaders sought a new raison d'être. They wanted to represent the "interests of the masses" in harmony with the "national interest," even if no independent, sectarian groups were to be allowed to exist.

At this point the negative question can be asked as to why "military fascism" in Japan was not brought about by a political party as in Germany, Italy, or elsewhere, and the more positive question as to why it was that the bureaucracy became the leading element in this transformation towards totalitarianism in Japan. Actually we shall only touch on the latter question in so far as it is necessary to answer the first, since we are discussing mainly the question of possible democratic participation of the people through political parties in prewar Japan. . . .

As we have seen, political parties, including the proletarian, constituted no more than a subsidiary means of control between the supra- and infra-structure of the "emperor system." Their squabbles were nothing more than competition to see which one or ones of them would play this role at any particular time. They were never able to overcome their internal bickering and transform themselves into one or more well organized mass parties on their own. And, of course, in such a power structure, the proletarian party was not able to grasp power in the role of a "fascist" party. Nevertheless, for a time "the normal path of constitutional government" was more or less operative, and certainly a possibility, which still leaves us with the question of why it was crushed under the weight of the bureaucratic forces. . . .

In the most general terms it can be said that "parliamentary rule," limited as it was, was nevertheless necessary to give the Japanese government the flexibility to withstand the changes taking place in a period of rapid industrial development and ideological turmoil. What concerned such conservative political leaders as Takahashi Korekiyo was not so much the giving in on universal suffrage as the maintenance of the traditional pattern of order on the local level. From about 1918 on, the landlord system was getting into real trouble, tenant-farmer disputes were on the increase, and the traditional village harmony (*ikka danraku*) was being broken. This village harmony, organized into what was misleadingly called "local self-government" (*chihō jichi*), formed the very foundation stones of the "emperor system." In order to restore this, the government, particularly from 1918 through 1924, gave special encouragement with funds and in other ways to local agricultural associations concerned with improving the farmers' livelihood through better information and techniques. By a revision of the Agricultural Association Law in 1922, over half of the farm households were forced to join the associations. Most noteworthy was the revision of the Industrial Guilds Law of 1932 which by a five-year plan was to place all these agricultural associations under the guilds as part of the "movement for the revitalization of the agricultural and fishing village economy," mentioned above. These *"Gemeindschaft"* associations, based on the local natural economy, were to be linked by the guilds, as *"Gesellschaften,"* to the larger industrial economy. Politically speaking, this was the way the reformist elements in the bureaucracy hoped to tie the local village order to the hem of the reformed "emperor system." This was at one with the bureaucracy's lending the authority of the government to the forced cartelization of the economy by the zaibatsu in the name of the "rationalization" of the economy. This was all part of the social, economic, and political reorganization brought about by the bureaucracy, starting around 1930, that essentially established "military fascism" in Japan. . . .

Through a number of laws and ordinances by the Home Ministry, neighborhood and block associations came under governmental regulation and formed the basic units for the Imperial Rule Assistance Association openly encouraging the local notables to take responsibility for local order and to become, through the local assemblies, the links to the totalitarianized state structure. . . .

In this revised social structure, the political parties lost their function of providing a link between the government and the people and this function was taken up instead by the many new organizations which organized the people down to the neighborhood and block associations and which were more amenable to bureaucratic control for mobilizing the whole country for war.

EVALUATION OF
JAPANESE DEMOCRATIC POTENTIALS

Economic Factors and Timing

ROBERT A. SCALAPINO

Earlier we have read Dr. Scalapino's account of the rise of capitalism in Japan and its social consequences. Now we can examine the way he compares this to other explanations of the failure of democracy in prewar Japan and what the implications of his own hypothesis are. He does not deny that democracy was tried in the prewar context but he holds that the very timing of the Japanese industrial revolution in world history precluded the possibility of internal forces arising strongly enough to challenge effectively the rise of military-bureaucratic rule.

The wider implications of this hypothesis suggest that the success of democracy in other, later-developing societies is not a foregone conclusion. Foreign aid may help to ease the transition of these societies into industrialism so that they do not have to resort to authoritarian methods. But Dr. Scalapino warns us that we shall have to become more discerning in detecting democratic potentials. If such societies adopt merely a façade of Western-style democratic institutions, they can deceive us unless we understand democracy in more dynamic terms. They must develop institutions that give expression to their own indigenous democratic forces and processes.

THE importance of understanding the failure of democracy in prewar Japan has never been greater than it is today. As a result of complete military defeat, Japan has been thrust upon the pathway of democracy a second time, but the future is . . . uncertain. Meanwhile, social change is the order of the day throughout Asia, with political forces and ideologies reaching a crescendo in battle. Obviously authoritarianism has countless advantages in this struggle, especially when it takes the modernized, dynamic form of Communism. The crucial and unanswered question is whether democracy can remove its legacy of failure everywhere in the Far East and demonstrate some capacity to survive and develop.

As a first step in exploring this possibility, it is essential to seek out the basic causes for past failures. In this work, we have attempted to focus on this problem in the context of Japan. If our conclusions are valid, however, it is possible that they may have a certain applicability to a much wider area. Like any society, of course, Japan has differences which make any complete identification with other communities impossible; indeed, Japanese "uniqueness" has been so widely heralded that this point scarcely need be made. In view of this, however, if it can be shown that some of

From Robert A. Scalapino, *Democracy and the Party Movement in Prewar Japan: The Failure of the First Attempt* (Berkeley, 1953), pp. 393–398. Reprinted by permission of the University of California Press.

the major causative factors involved in the failure of Japanese democracy were the result not of "uniqueness" but of certain "similarities," then they assume an enhanced significance. There is another advantage in studying Japan in an effort to discern the most basic handicaps facing democracy in late-developing societies. In some respects, Japan resembles a "controlled experiment." The presumed prerequisites for a modern democratic society — the independent nation-state, industrialization, and mass literacy — were all attained by modern Japan. Thus one is not dealing with a society which lacked the elementary democratic "requirements." Furthermore, one is examining a society which reached goals now common to almost all "underdeveloped" areas and therefore a society which might represent in some degree their projected future.

Before seeking to relate the Japanese prewar experience with democracy to broader horizons, however, it is necessary to present some generalizations concerning that experience. Certainly there can be no doubt that democracy failed in prewar Japan, but our major effort throughout this study has been to find the most basic reasons for that failure. It is possible, of course, to argue that democracy was never really tried in Japan, but that is to beg the question. It received the only kind of trial which Japanese society was equipped to give it. It failed, moreover, in an atmosphere of world failure, with democracy losing ground in many diverse parts of the globe.

One "explanation" that frequently dominates an analysis of this problem is the "plot" thesis. In its overextended use, this thesis carries the implication that Japanese democracy was born with the promise of a long and fruitful life, but was throttled in its infancy by the machinations of evil men. . . . [S]uch an explanation for the failure of Japanese democracy can only be superficial. Japan, to be sure, had its full share of Machiavellian leaders and men of ill will. Moreover, as we have seen, some of her greatest and most dedicated statesmen

were extremly clever at placing additional obstacles in front of democracy. But it is vital to realize that in the case of Japanese society, there were impersonal forces operating both within and outside in such a fashion as to establish a steeply graded table of probability with regard to social change. The more central explanation for the failure of the Japanese democratic movement must be found within these forces.

Perhaps the most orthodox and widely accepted explanation for the failure of democracy in Japan has revolved around Japanese tradition or culture. The incompatibility between Japanese tradition and democracy has been recognized in both the East and the West, and this theme has been expressed in a great variety of ways. Even the casual observer can see the differences between the West and Japan at the close of the nineteenth century. . . .

When one deals with "cultural differences," however, there are many questions to be asked and certain problems left unsolved. Some of these questions quite naturally go far beyond the subject of Japan or the Far East. Prominent among those cultural elements of the West to which the evolution of democracy has been attributed are Greek humanism, the Hebraic-Christian philosophy, and Roman law. There is very strong evidence to indicate that these played some role in the later development of modern democratic thought and institutions, although Western students are by no means agreed upon the precise contributions which each made. It is extremely interesting to note, however, that the "cultural differences" between the medieval West and the Far East of that same period did not preclude a similarity of basic values, with their respective major themes almost indistinguishable.

The medieval Western ideal was that of organic unity and the integration of all concepts into a single, harmonious whole. These themes predominated in medieval institutions and thought, despite certain clear evidences of pluralism, evidences which could of course be paralleled in the Far East. There was no place for non-conformity or individualism — no place for theories of accepted differences or competitive ideas. . . .

The emphasis of the medieval West upon organic unity and its preoccupation with the search for complete synthesis was in substantial accord with the dominant themes of "the great harmony" and organic integration which prevailed in the Far East. There was no complete identity, to be sure, and there were stirrings in the West, most of them connected with the titanic struggle between church and state, which had significant implications for the future. But the similarity of ideals between the West and East during this period cannot be denied, and behind this lay a similarity in political-economic institutions. In neither area were the dominant philosophical chords those of democratic theory, although it is possible to find some embryonic potentialities in both. And one should not forget that the medieval West had already had some considerable heritage of Greek humanism, Hebraic-Christian philosophy, and Roman law.

Then when did the profound differences between such societies as nineteenth-century England and Japan emerge, and what produced them? It seems obvious that whatever their seeds in the medieval period, they were centrally connected with the great developments which led up to and included the Western industrial revolution. The emergence of modern democracy cannot be separated from the early rise of capitalism within the framework of the nation-state. In England, this process was in operation from the Tudor period onward, although many stages were involved. And with this process was connected not only an increasing differentiation between West and East, but also one between various parts of the West.

The fact that it took something more than a cultural legacy of humanism, Roman law, and Hebraic-Christian philosophy to make modern democracy is revealed in

a striking manner both by the medieval period of European history and by the evolution of the modern West itself. Western political evolution, indeed, offers some very important evidence relating to the Japanese problem. The readers of this study have seen the remarkable political parallels between the modern societies of Japan and Germany. Certainly these were not the result of a common cultural tradition in the sense in which this concept is usually understood. Germany had been subjected to the great forces of Western tradition mentioned above. The factor that connected Japan and Germany was not tradition but the timing of their "modernization."

This factor of timing not only helps to explain the similarities between these two societies, but also offers a central explanation for the failure of democracy in both. To retrace our steps somewhat, it seems clear that "cultures" change, at least if the central values of a society are any index to its culture. The differences between the dominant ideals of the Western medieval period and those of the Western liberal society of the nineteenth century were profound. Behind these differences was the change from feudalism to the modern capitalist state. It is undoubtedly true that the great forces in Western tradition played an important role in inducing this change. However, a host of other factors were involved, including many which were far from deterministic in character. As a result, certain areas which had shared the broadest traditions of the West lagged behind in this new phase. Where the lag was appreciable, it could produce very substantial differences in the political forms of modern industrial-centered societies. Essentially, these variations all reflected the rational interests of commercial-industrial classes. In short, the industrial revolution was conducive to more than one political expression, depending upon the timing and intensity of its development. In the case of many late arrivals, the doctrines of economic and political liberalism were not the most logical expression of industrialism. Thus many aspects of the preindustrial heritage were little changed, not only because of the speed of the transition but also because the newly emerging forces did not present a strong challenge.

How do these hypotheses apply to modern Japan? They certainly do not imply that the traditional heritage of that society was unimportant in the modern period, but they do suggest that its real force came from the degree to which it harmonized with the requirements of a late-developing industrial society. There is no need to summarize in any detail the evidence presented earlier in this study which supports such a thesis. As we have seen, the inability of Japanese capitalism to underwrite the cardinal principles of democracy was centrally connected with the timing of its development, as this related to conditions both in Japan and in the world. This fact, in turn, had a direct or indirect influence upon every facet of modern Japan. The power of agrarianism, the history of Japanese constitutionalism, the character of Japanese nationalism — all were vitally affected. . . .

If timing does represent the major explanation for the failure of democracy in Japan, the ramifications of this fact can be very broad. Western-style democracy is the product of an earlier evolution which cannot possibly be duplicated in the modern world. The "natural evolution" of the same forces which molded eighteenth- and nineteenth-century England and the United States will not produce parallel results in the twentieth century. But this does not necessarily mean that the democratic cause is lost. It does mean that new techniques

and ideas will have to be applied in order to adjust democracy to the modern world.

First, this involves the acceptance of a concept of democracy which is not burdened with provincialism or an inelastic historic reference and yet incorporates the indispensable essence of the democratic system. Perhaps the definition of democracy given in . . . this study is serviceable in these respects. That definition established two criteria: (1) adherence to the concept of the innate dignity of man and recognition of his total development as the ultimate goal of the state; and (2) acceptance of choice as the fundamental qualification of democratic institutions, with positive protection for civil liberties, a competitive party system, and the other necessities of an "open society." Such a definition acknowledges by implication the need for economic-political experimentation and recognizes the diversity of existing types of democratic societies. . . .

How democracy is defined and philosophically defended is tremendously important today, and especially in an area like the Far East. In many respects, this is an age attuned to faith, when men everywhere are searching for ideals and programs which will give them hope and courage and, at the same time, relate them and their society to the rest of the world. The fact that Communism has captured much of the democratic symbolism and dynamic appeal in certain parts of Asia and among certain Asian groups is in part a commentary upon the narrow and paradoxical connotations which some of its "supporters" have foisted upon democracy.

Cultural Continuity

CHITOSHI YANAGA

While economic and technological innovations can change the face of a society, it is certainly possible that traditional modes of thought may only readjust to these changes without themselves undergoing transformation. Further, if those cultural traits are fundamentally nonequalitarian and antidemocratic, is there then much hope for the development of genuine democracy without a social revolution taking place in that society? Dr. Yanaga does not think so.

Few people are as well qualified as Dr. Yanaga to assess the inner workings of Japanese psychology. Born in Hawaii and raised in a bilingual and bicultural environment, he took his Ph.D. at the University of California at Berkeley in 1934 and then studied at Tōkyō Imperial University from 1935 to 1937. His *Japan Since Perry*, based on Japanese sources, is one of the most detailed and erudite histories of modern Japan written in English. The present selection is taken from a study made well after the end of the American occupation. His postwar examination of Japanese politics evidently convinced him that democracy in prewar Japan was more of a façade than a groundwork for postwar development.

THE constitutional parliamentary system launched in 1890 operated in a singularly Japanese fashion. Westernization in the political sphere at best was little more than a superficial imitation of European and American institutions which had been transplanted only in so far as their structural features were concerned, and the adoption of Western political language or, rather, political nomenclature. The Japanese leaders did not wish to go much further in their modernization. This resulted in a multiplicity of façades which served to obscure if not conceal, especially for the casual or superficial observer, the traditional concepts and attitudes that were much too deeply rooted in the nation's past to be readily superseded by alien ideas and ways of doing things. In other words, Westernization which was carried out assiduously as part of the national program of modernization in the 1870's and 1880's without any compulsion from the outside, was never given the opportunity to undergo full and unrestricted development.

The forced modernization of the nation was inevitably accompanied by distortion, if not perversion, of values. For example, on the one hand there was an almost excessive emphasis on the good of the nation, that is, the national strength and prosperity, while on the other too little attention was paid to the well-being of the individual as a whole. The solution of problems which were producing the serious stresses and strains, as for example in the 1870's, was not worked out internally but sought and obtained in expansion. In this process attention was diverted from internal to external problems. The people, in spite of their own economic plight and oppressive restraints, deluded themselves into

From Chitoshi Yanaga, *Japanese People and Politics* (New York, 1956), pp. 4–5, 30–31, and 34–38. Reprinted by permission of John Wiley and Sons.

thinking that the prosperity of the nation was synonymous with their own individual prosperity.

Japan's modernization actually plunged the nation from feudalism into an expansionist state without the benefit of a transitional period of bourgeois society which might have developed liberal tendencies. . . .

In political ideas and practices Westernization [even today] has not proceeded as far or as deeply as a casual observer of the political scene is wont to conclude especially when conclusions are based on what he perceives only physically. A visitor to the Diet will see the members dressed in Western clothes deliberating in a modern building of modified Arabic architecture and conducting themselves according to rules of procedure which are more likely than not based upon the rules of order employed in the Congress of the United States. He is impressed by the resemblance between them and the members of Congress.

The truth of the matter is that the resemblances are superficial at best. What goes on in the minds of the Japanese M.P.'s are quite different both in substance and in the process by which they take shape. In their ideas and their mode of thought and action they are still far more Japanese than meets the eye, in spite of their apparent Westernization. Moreover, many Western concepts and practices have been so greatly modified to serve their purpose that in some instances they have been changed beyond recognition, just as has been done, in the course of centuries, with the importations or borrowings from China, India, and other parts of the world.

It is undeniable that Westernization has gone very far where individuals are concerned, especially in their technological training. Those who are highly trained as engineers, chemists, physicists, or mathematicians are completely Western in their scientific methods and thinking within the fields of their professional competence. However, as human beings and members of a social group, their Westernization is negligible for they are quite naturally Japanese. There is no appreciable transfer of scientific thought and attitude over into the realm of social relations, attitudes, and standards.

Westernization then could be achieved only within, and to the extent tolerated by, the framework of social structure and traditional thought patterns. Consequently it has been more successful in borrowing the forms than the spirit or substance even where genuine and assiduous efforts have been made. Furthermore national aspirations and goals and political considerations have frequently served as effective brakes to Westernization.

The Western impact has been most evident and significant along material, scientific, and technological lines. Visible and appraisable effects have been largely in such matters as organization, procedures, production techniques, management, and finance, and very little in the nonmaterial and spiritual aspects of national life. To illustrate this in the military development: the most modern scientific weapons were adopted by the armed forces and effective organization was used as witnessed in the Pacific War, and yet scientific thinking so far as psychology was concerned was virtually undeveloped. For all the modern weapons used, what existed in the minds of the military was not twentieth century scientific warfare but feudal samurai psychology which was responsible for the suicidal banzai charges which contributed nothing toward winning the war, the Kamikaze attacks which were, at best, of dubious value, and such fantastic ideas as fighting with bamboo spears.

Thus the Japanese have mastered science and technology as well as many of the advanced nations of the West and better than a good many of the less advanced Western countries. But the social ideas, structure, and environment in which they have found application have not undergone sufficient changes to accommodate technological advances in a Western manner.

This situation obtains because Japanese society has not really been subjected to penetrating stresses or upheavals such as would shake it to its very foundation. No foreign invader at any time foisted an alien culture upon the people. Nor has there been anything comparable to the Renaissance which altered the nature of Western society. Actually spiritual development in Japan was introverted to the extent that it was conditioned entirely by her own spiritual needs for centuries. Some segments of the Japanese people have at various times completely yielded to foreign influences, like the French who are particularly fond of ideas and are easily carried away, but the nation as a whole, like the English people, has remained conservative. . . .

*   *   *

In the second half of the nineteenth century the new Japanese intellectuals read avidly and enthusiastically the works of political economists and political philosophers of the West. Writings of Ricardo, Adam Smith, Jeremy Bentham, John Stuart Mill, Montesquieu, J. J. Rousseau, and Alexis de Tocqueville were practically devoured by the politically ambitious and the intellectuals of the early Meiji period especially in the 1870's and 1880's. Utilitarianism, economic liberalism, and laissez-faire were espoused. But there were serious limitations and obstacles which stood in the way of the development of true liberalism.

Always Japanese liberalism was subservient to the interests of the state and overshadowed by statism and could exist only to the extent tolerated or permitted by the state. Furthermore, it was never based on individualism for this did not exist. Its fatal weakness lay in the fact that liberalism was adopted in form but not really in principle. This was largely the result of the eagerness to impress and convince the Western powers that Japan had risen to their level. It was not an adoption of its substance which was understood by the people and desired by them. Furthermore, it was made a

weapon or instrument, a sort of expedient, of power struggle against the clan oligarchy.

Japanese liberalism was developed in an abnormal and distored form and overrated by those who wrote about it later without a careful study of the realities of the movement. Western liberalism as transplanted in Japan was devoid of philosophy and principles, stripped of liberty, and without economic liberalism. If indeed there has begun a bourgeois revolution, the process has not been completed. To this fact may be partially attributed the presence of vestiges of strong authoritarianism if not absolutism as an element of political life.

The Confucian canon of decorum is so firmly embedded in social life and consciousness it not only takes precedence over liberty but actually works to check it. To an individual it is normally more important to be proper and conforming than to be right according to his convictions. Confucianism, which served as an instrument of thought control throughout the greater part of Chinese history and during the Tokugawa period of Japanese history, was actually used by the Japanese government and individuals as an effective antidote to Western ideas, especially liberalism, in the last two decades of the nineteenth century, for some of the influential leaders deemed liberalism and democracy to be antithetical to kokutai [national polity]. It must be emphasized, however, that in spite of unfavorable conditions a considerable number of individuals of liberal convictions appeared on the scene.

Liberty, equality, and fraternity which were borrowed from the French enjoyed tremendous popularity, but again what really happened was that most of the people were fascinated by the sound of the political slogan without being influenced by the substance of the ideas. In other words, while they were virtually shouted from the housetops and enjoyed wide currency, they did not actually develop into a vital force in the political life of the nation. To many, even today, liberty seems to connote something uncontrolled, undisciplined, licentious, and even uncivilized.

Equality was nonexistent in a class-ordered society such as Japan. Conditions more conducive to the development of equality appear to have existed in primitive society before the introduction of Chinese civilization. However, for practically the entire span of Japan's historic period, inequality both in concept and practice has been the normal condition of society. The same thing can be said with respect to the equality of sexes.

Egalitarianism, therefore, is a Western contribution which has only very slowly developed in the face of traditional forces which still condition if not regulate social and political behavior. The inordinate respect and deference shown to individuals on the basis of age, rank, and status, and even occupation, as well as the particular relationships, make the road to equality a rough one indeed. Even the matter of equality of women, which has been legally established in the Constitution itself, can be realized only when the traditional forces have been liquidated or neutralized.

In the political ideas of the Japanese today, there is a conspicuous overlay of Western ideas on traditional concepts. At the same time there has also been a hybridization of ideas, political, economic, and social. In few areas of political activity is this characteristic so much in evidence as in the socialist movement. As a Western inspired movement it was completely Western in its ideological content. It was only natural that the theory of socialism should be superimposed upon Japanese ideological foundations resulting in an overlay without radically changing indigenous ideas. Wherever modifications took place in the ideas, the results were more in the nature of hybridization than of complete assimilation.

There has been since World War I a decided Marxian bias among Japanese intellectuals particularly in the universities. In the 1920's Marxism had completely captured the imagination of Japanese intellectuals. Not only had it become intellectually fashionable to believe in Marxism, but anyone who did not show his understanding of as well as enthusiasm for it was regarded as lacking in intellectual capacity. This attitude stems from the fact that the Japanese have always shown a peculiar "weakness" or predilection for theory and for neat theoretical statements deductively arrived at. In the dialectical materialism offered by Marxism and the "scientific" reasoning it contained, they found a special irresistible fascination.

The Japanese have not developed a strong sense of contrast between the real and the ideal. This enables them to overlook the real by concentrating on the ideal. It is quite possible that the intellectuals indulged themselves increasingly in theoretical mental exercises as the door was closed on practical and empirical examination and study particularly of economic and political matters. As a matter of fact the government encouraged theoretical emphasis in political science so that the studies carried on by the scholars were almost all highly legalistic and theoretical. Constitutional law was a subject of exigetical study without any reference to politics or actual government. In the universities there were no courses on Japanese government and politics; instead there were courses on the Constitution.

America's intensive campaign "to make the world safe for democracy" during World War I stirred the imagination of students and produced unexpected repercussions in Japan. War against Germany came to be regarded as a crusade against autocracy and the forces of tyranny which were symbolized by the Kaiser. The undreamed-of economic prosperity that was produced by the war was somehow associated with democracy and aided the popularity of democratic ideas and ideals. In this upsurge of democratic idealism, Professor Yoshino of Tokyo Imperial University was the leading exponent. Under his influence came scores of students who became exponents of liberalism and democracy and subsequently leaders of pro-

98

letarian political movements. Out of the student population of World War I and after came the leaders of the socialist movement. Some of them turned Communists soon after the Bolshevik Revolution of 1917 which had a tremendous impact in Japan.

Extreme vulnerability to boredom is one of the characteristics of the Japanese, notably among the educated and the intellectuals. This, combined with the intellectuals' special susceptibity to frustrations and their identification of their interests with those of the working class and the shifting of their mood from intense dedication to intense boredom, has undoubtedly contributed greatly to the appearance of radical ideas and movements in Japan.

It has been repeatedly said that Japanese political changes almost never assume clearcut swings of the pendulum and that they are almost always blurred compromises. There is a great deal of truth in such a characterization, for the Japanese may well agree with the French that the more the situation changes the more it remains the same, that there have been almost no radical reformers in history who have been successful, and that traditionally the ideal path for one to follow has been the middle way. Going to extremes has been frowned upon for not only does it introduce discord and conflict but it would be considered highly aberrant.

There have been reforms, renovations, and restorations but no revolutions in Japanese history. Actually the only type of revolution the Japanese are familiar with is the palace revolution which involves merely a change in the group in power either in a peaceful and almost imperceptible manner or in a coup d'etat. Political revolution in the Western sense involving a change in the location of sovereignty or an upheaval in social organization resulting in the destruction of the old order and the establishment of a new social order had never really occurred. Even a dynastic "revolution" is unknown in Japan. Taine's characterization of England as a nation which lends itself to reform without yielding itself to revolution might well be applied to Japan.

Similarity of Problems in Japan and the West

EDWIN O. REISCHAUER

Since the experts on modern Japanese history are agreed on when and where most specific events occurred, why do they differ so much on their interpretations of democratic potentials in Japan? This is a very difficult question. So far we have seen that differences of emphases are related to differences of the interpretation of democracy. If one emphasizes the economic environment in which the society is developing, as Dr. Scalapino did, the political process itself can be considered of less importance. If one stresses the psychological aspects, as Dr. Yananga has done, then traditional modes of thought rank as more important than borrowed institutions. But if outward behavior is to be considered crucial, as it can be argued Dr. Reischauer believes, the institutions of voting and parliamentary deliberation rank high in the estimation of the degree of democracy that has existed and does exist in Japan.

All the authors represented here, outside of Dr. Reischauer, consider that the feudal heritage has dampened, if not stifled, democratic development. In contrast, while not denying the undemocratic characteristics of feudalism as such, Dr. Reischauer argues that feudalism with its emphasis on decentralization, contractual relationships, and rivalry among groups, actually provided Japan with a background similar to that which in Europe produced both capitalism and democracy. As Dr. Reischauer sees it, a similar type of feudalism did not exist elsewhere in Asia. Thus Japan had a background that could help it modernize more rapidly than any other Asian society.

One further important element in his analysis, however, is that modernization does not necessarily lead to democracy; it can equally well lead to "totalitarianism" because of the new techniques of control that have been developed. He sees a struggle between the forces of democracy and totalitarianism of one form or another going on in all modern societies. In this sense Japan is just as much in the mainstream of the modern world as any of the other advanced countries.

Any account of the Japanese which gives the impression that theirs is an unchangeable or even unchanging society would be extremely misleading. All the major cultures of the world, at least in modern times, have been characterized by a rapid and, it would seem, accelerating rate of change. . . .

Japan in the past hundred years has witnessed not just superficial modifications but a fundamental social as well as economic and political transformation. Many students of the Far East have held that Japan has borrowed only the outer forms of Western civilization but has failed to understand or appreciate the inner content of our culture, and they even contrast the superficiality of Japanese Westernization with the more basic influences the Occident is said to have had on other Asiatic countries.

Behind this theory is the contrast between the Japanese intellectuals of today and many of the intellectuals of China and India, for instance. The Japanese, though thoroughly familiar with the history, philosophy, and literature of the West, has received his education in the Japanese language in Japanese schools and universities, whereas his Chinese or Indian counterpart, in so far as he is well versed in Occidental lore, probably has received a good part of his education in the English language and some of it in the Occident. The linguistic barrier, if nothing else, makes the Japanese intellectual seem less Westernized than the Indian or Chinese. But this is no measure of the degree of Westernization in these lands. The Japanese receives his training about the West as part of a normal Japanese education. The Indian or Chinese must go outside of his native culture to learn much about the West. . . .

The very idea that there is a distinction between the outer forms and the inner content of a civilization is a curious misconception. The Meiji leaders may have had this misconception too; they probably never dreamed how profoundly their reforms would remake the Japanese people. Of course, Japan remains in many ways essentially Japanese, and yet industrialization, universal education, and all the other external innovations from the West could not leave the Japanese basically unchanged. The Oxford-trained Indian and the Chinese with a Columbia Ph.D. may be more obviously Westernized than the graduate in English literature from Tokyo University, who, though well read in Shakespeare and Milton, has never been abroad or even had many opportunities to speak English, but the Japanese people from Cabinet Minister down to the humblest peasant have been influenced by the West in a way that is entirely unknown among the masses of India or China.

A great deal is heard today of the titanic social revolution which is beginning to sweep Asia, but it should be remembered that the initial convulsions of this conti-

nent-shaking revolution swept through the Japanese islands decades ago. The nationalistic awakening, industrialization, the spread of education, the revolutionary concept that the common man should participate in and perhaps even control government, all hit Japan long before the rest of Asia, but, perhaps because of some basic difference in the underlying geologic formations of society, the upheaval was less destructive in the islands than on the continent and passed almost unnoticed by the rest of the world. Japan for long has been a thoroughly nationalistic country; she has already made her adjustment to the machine age; her society has been transformed by universal education; and the Japanese have had a longer history of encouraging successes and disheartening failures in the field of representative government than any other people in Asia. While most of the rest of Asia is being shaken to the core by these same forces and the ultimate outcome is far from clear, Japanese society has adjusted quickly and easily, yielding to the force of the upheaval the way the light, frame buildings of Japan move with the motion of an earthquake, instead of standing rigid until cracked and thrown to the ground like the brick walls of China.

But these were only the initial shocks of the temblor. Japan weathered them gallantly, only to be faced with the new and even more complex problems of an industrialized and modernized state, such as face the countries of Europe. The clashes of contemporary Japan, while carrying Asiatic overtones, are basically not unlike the discords of modern Europe. Her problems find a closer parallel in England or Italy and still more perhaps in Germany than in neighboring China or Korea.

It seems safe to assume that the other lands of Asia, too, will find their present travail simply a prelude to new and equally difficult problems. The Japanese experience should make it clear that industrialization and universal education, however necessary or desirable they may be, offer no panacea for Asia. But the Japanese experience can certainly not be taken as any exact forecast of future developments in the rest of Asia. The very speed of the early stages of the revolution in Japan shows that there are fundamental differences between her and her Asiatic neighbors — differences which may affect their respective courses in the future as much as they have during the past hundred years.

Many have explained the greater speed of the Japanese reaction to the Western impact as a result of Japan's smallness and insular position, which made her more susceptible to rapid physical penetration by Western influences than were the vast stretches of China's landlocked interior provinces. This geographic factor, however, was probably not the major one. More important were Japan's ready acceptance of the concept of borrowing from abroad, her long established nationalism, her experience during feudal times with legal concepts somewhat similar to those of the West, and other basic points of resemblance to Europe. Japan in the early nineteenth century, far from having achieved the monolithic ideal of China, actually came closed to approximating the early modern states of Europe in her multiple authorities and her social as well as political diversity. She had also laid a firmer foundation than China for the development of a capitalistic economy, which, together with nationalism, serves as a cornerstone of modern Western civilization.

Japanese feudalism, in theory, had no more room for capitalism than had the feudalism of Europe, and yet Japanese feudal lords and retainers were heavily in debt to capitalistic moneylenders, and the feudal realms financed themselves by selling their surplus rice in a national market and by collaborating with businessmen in setting up trade or production monopolies. Many feudal realms maintained financial agents at Osaka to sell their rice and arrange for necessary purchases. The great rice markets at Osaka and Edo, with their dealings in futures and their delicately synchronized fluctuations in prices, closely resembled the major wheat markets of postfeudal Western Europe. The influence of the Chinese attitude of contempt for trade and the trader had strengthened Japanese feudal prejudices, resulting in the preposterous theory that the merchant class was the lowest social grouping, but in reality the city merchants dominated not only the economy but also the literature and art of the late Tokugawa period. Culturally a bourgeois revolution had already taken place in Japan, and the economy, despite the feudal façade, was in many ways an early capitalistic economy, not unlike that of Western Europe in early modern times.

Small wonder then that the Japanese rapidly adopted and exploited the capitalistic practices of the West. Small rural entrepreneurs quickly saw the advantages of capital investments to mechanize silk reeling and thus created Japan's first truly successful export industry; merchants cautiously converted their enterprises into modern banking or merchandising firms; and former feudal lords and samurai used their government bonds to become modern industrialists and bankers. While the capital of China for the most part remained tied by tradition and governmental caprice to the land or to short-term investments, Japanese capitalists were building up some of the greatest economic empires the world has ever seen.

Why the Japanese alone among the peoples of the eastern periphery of the Old World had these basic resemblances to the peoples of the western periphery is not a question which can be easily answered, nor has anyone seriously sought to answer it. Certain possible explanations, however, suggest themselves as worthy of further study. For one thing, Japan resembles Western Europe geographically and climatically more than do the other countries of Asia, with the single exception of her close neighbor, Korea. Even more significant is the complex of fundamental traits which followed one another in somewhat the same order in both Japan and Europe. Appearing independently of each other at the two opposite ends of the Old World, these parallel groupings and sequences of cultural characteristics suggest interesting causal relationships. Behind nationalism and an at least incipient capitalism in both areas lay a feudal experience, which in fundamental characteristics was amazingly similar in Japan and Europe; and behind feudalism lay the meeting in each case of an aristocratic, tribal society with a universal religion of salvation and a classic civilization which stressed a unified, authoritarian state. In most of Western Europe the tribesmen absorbed some of the classic civilization in the process of conquering and destroying it. In Japan they imbibed deeper draughts of the classic civilization by the more unusual procedure of consciously importing it to their own land. The process was different, but the basic ingredients were by no means wholly dissimilar.

Thus, behind Japan's spectacular Westernization in recent years lay earlier resemblances to the West. Perhaps Japan is not merely the most Westernized land of Asia but is more significantly the most "Western" land of Asia. It is fundamentally and unmistakably a cultural daughter of China — an integral part of the civilization of the Far East — but at the same time it has been the country which has diverged the most consistently and markedly from Far Eastern norms, and these points of difference have been, by and large, points of basic resemblance to the West.

If this is true, then it is not surprising that Japan, in contrast to the rest of Asia, survived the initial shock of the Western impact with relative ease, only to run headlong into the problems which grip the West today. These are not only the economic problems of the industrialized and specialized economies. . . . A vastly more difficult problem which Westernization has brought Japan . . . has been the clash, or perhaps more properly the conflicting pull, of the two great forces produced by the modern techniques of machine production and universal education — the pull toward greater individual freedom, toward intellectual independence and democratic political rights, and the often conflicting pull toward a stricter integration of society, toward governmental controls over economy, and enforced totalitarian uniformity.

We lack terms both comprehensive and precise enough to describe this sharply drawn and pervasive struggle within modern civilization. Perhaps "democracy" and "totalitarianism" come closest to being the terms we need, but both convey too little in exact scope and at the same time too much in emotional overtones. But the clash exists and nowhere more clearly than in Japan. It is surprising how quickly and strongly these two forces manifested themselves in Japan after the introduction of Western ideas and techniques and how completely they dominate the history of modern Japan. In fact, modern Japanese history can be interpreted without great distortion primarily in terms of a curiously ambivalent and fitful progress in these two different directions and growing swings of the pendulum between these two roads of simultaneous advance as they increasingly diverged from each other. . . .

The strange multi-cornered struggle in prewar Japan between army officers, civil bureaucrats, *zaibatsu* executives, party politicians, terroristic demagogues, and liberal intellectuals offers a uniquely Japanese picture, but, after all the curious Oriental detail, such as Shinto mumbo-jumbo, "Imperial will," and samurai prestige, have been removed, the stark outlines of the picture bear an all too clear resemblance to the major outlines of Western history in recent decades. In fact, the Japanese picture perhaps helps to sharpen our own myopic vision and enable us to see behind the bewildering surface patterns of intense nationalistic rivalries the outlines of the titanic struggle between the forces of democracy and totalitarianism in our own half of the world — and for that matter wherever the complexities of machine production have resulted in high standards of popular education and the close integration of society on a national scale. The conflict is not always so clear-cut or so evenly balanced as it was in prewar Japan, but it exists in some form or another throughout the whole political spectrum of the modern world. The extreme integration of society in the modern totalitarian state depends on education, and education inevitably tends to breed the desire for individual freedom. On the other hand, education and the economic basis for individual freedom as we know it today depend on the extreme integration of an industrialized society, and integration in turn tends to produce limitations on individual freedom. The strongly democratic lands of the West all show a rapid and apparently irresistible drift toward greater governmental controls over individual freedom of action, while each totalitarian regime ostentatiously maintains a show of democratic electoral procedures and is vociferous about its democratic aims. The point of conflict is different, but the nature of the conflict is basically the same. The two forces of democracy and totalitarianism are inevitable concomitants of machine production and universal education, and their harmonious reconciliation is no easy matter.

The struggle between democracy and totalitarianism was not merely a passing phase of prewar Japanese history. The fires of war and the surgery of defeat have brought physical and spiritual changes within the body politic of Japan, but this fundamental struggle goes on.

SUGGESTIONS FOR ADDITIONAL READING

The purpose of this bibliographical note is to mention a few of the more important and accessible books in English — and an even smaller number of articles — which deal directly or indirectly with the democratic trends in prewar Japan. A handy general bibliography is Hugh Borton *et al*, compilers, *A Selected List of Books and Articles on Japan in English, French and German* (Revised and enlarged — Cambridge, Mass., 1954). Even more convenient, because it is a brief paperback, is the interpretative bibliography by John Whitney Hall, *Japanese History: New Dimensions of Approach and Understanding* (Service Center for Teachers of History, Publication Number 34 — Washington, D. C., 1961).

The most detailed and accurate single volume on the history of modern Japan from just prior to the Meiji Restoration to the first years of the Allied Occupation is Chitoshi Yanaga's *Japan Since Perry* (New York, 1949). In addition to a bibliography of works in Western languages, it has a fairly comprehensive one of books in Japanese for those students who are embarking on the adventure of learning the Japanese language, an endeavor which has recently been facilitated by the publication of new learning materials and the greater availability of courses. Many of the other recent studies mentioned below also have fine bibliographies and extremely helpful indexes for finding material on specific persons or events. One of these is another, somewhat shorter, history of the same period with somewhat greater emphasis on external relations: Hugh Borton, *Japan's Modern Century* (New York, 1955). The most recent full-length study is W. G. Beasley, *The Modern History of Japan* (New York, 1963), which concentrates on the political aspects of modernization. Edwin O. Reischauer has revised

and brought up to date his *Japan: Past and Present* (New York, 1946; Third edition, revised, 1964). Also his *The United States and Japan* (Cambridge, Mass., 1950) treats in detail problems of especial significance for Americans, but one must not be misled by the title: this is really a history of modern Japan. A revised edition of this appeared in 1957 and a paperback Compass Book Edition was published in 1962.

Other recent paperbacks include: Richard Storry, *A History of Modern Japan* (A Pelican Book, 1960); Arthur Tiedemann, *Modern Japan: A Brief History* (An Anvil Original, 1955; revised and enlarged, 1962); and Sir Esler Dening, *Japan* (Praeger Paperbacks, 1960). The first is a general history; the second contains a series of readings from important documents; and the third is devoted largely to the postwar period.

For readings in Japanese intellectual history, the most comprehensive recent collection is Ryusaku Tsunoda, Wm. Theodore de Bary, and Donald Keene, compilers, *Sources of the Japanese Tradition* (New York, 1958). Of most relevance to our topic is Part Five: "Japan and the West," contributed to by Marius Jansen, Hyman Kublin, Arthur Tiedemann, Herschel Webb, Masao Abe, John F. Howes, and George O. Totten. This deals with liberalism, socialism, and nationalism in its various forms, as well as other religious and cultural trends in modern Japanese thought. A two-volume paperback edition of this appeared in 1964.

A series of essays on the development of modern Japan by contemporary Japanese authorities is found in Shigenobu Ōkuma, compiler, *Fifty Years of New Japan* (*Kaikoku Gojūnen Shi*), English version edited by Marcus B. Huish, 2 vols. (London, 1909–10). Another series is edited by Kaikoku Hyakunen Kinen Bunka Jigyō Kai

(Centenary Culture Council) under the general title *Japanese Culture in the Meiji Era*. Of especial relevance is Vol. 7: *Outline of Japanese History in the Meiji Era*, by Fujii Jintarō, translated by Hattie K. and Kenneth E. Colton (1958); Vol. 9: *Japanese Thought in the Meiji Era*, by Kōsaka Masaaki, translated by David Abosch (1958); and Vol. 10: *Japanese Legislation in the Meiji Era*, by Ishii Ryōsuke, translated by W. J. Chambliss (1958).

Among the more readable prewar accounts of the liberal movement in Meiji Japan are two by Japanese: Uichi Iwasaki, *The Working Forces in Japanese Politics: A Brief Account of Political Conflicts, 1867–1920* (New York, 1921) and Yusuke Tsurumi, "The Liberal Movement in Japan" and "The Origin and Growth of the Labor Movement in Japan" in Sir Valentine Chirol, Yusuke Tsurumi, and Sir James Arthur Salter, *The Reawakening of the Orient and Other Addresses* (New Haven, 1925).

A prewar account of Taishō democracy is available in A. Morgan Young, *Japan in Recent Times, 1912–26* (New York, 1929). The author was a Western journalist with a strong concern for democratic trends. He followed this with the less satisfactory *Imperial Japan, 1926–1938* (New York, 1939) which nevertheless communicates the fear for democracy and for the future of Japan felt by an eyewitness. The most comprehensive prewar academic study of Japanese government by a Westerner was Harold S. Quigley's *Japanese Government and Politics: An Introductory Study* (New York, 1932). More interpretive, though perhaps somewhat overdrawn, is *Japan, Government-Politics* (New York, 1939) by Robert Karl Reischauer (the brother of Edwin O. Reischauer — who was killed in the Japanese attack on Shanghai in 1937).

As a forerunner of the more scholarly and sophisticated postwar monographs on aspects of modern Japanese history, E.

Herbert Norman produced a most suggestive study in *Japan's Emergence as a Modern State: Political and Economic Problems of the Meiji Period* (New York, 1940). One of the first whose ability in the Japanese language enabled him to become thoroughly familiar with the work of Japanese scholars and actual source materials, he was followed by Nobutaka Ike who wrote *The Beginnings of Political Democracy in Japan* (Baltimore, 1950). This study in turn helped inspire George M. Beckmann to write *The Making of the Meiji Constitution: The Oligarchs and the Constitutional Development of Japan, 1868–1891* (Lawrence, Kansas, 1957). Finally, the most comprehensive monograph to focus on the question of democracy in prewar Japan is Robert A. Scalapino, *Democracy and the Party Movement in Prewar Japan: The Failure of the First Attempt* (Berkeley and Los Angeles, 1953).

Of more specialized monographs, one that plays down the critical character of the conflict between the Meiji oligarchs and the advocates of parliamentary government is George Akita, *Foundations of Constitutional Government in Modern Japan, 1868–1900* (Cambridge, Mass., 1965). The subsequent changes in constitutional interpretation until the mid-1930's are covered in the study of Yoshino Sakuzō's teacher by Frank O. Miller, *Minobe Tatsukichi: Interpreter of Constitutionalism in Japan* (Berkeley and Los Angeles, 1965).

For the role of the proletarian parties, their leadership, and organized support, see George Oakley Totten, III, *The Social Democratic Movement in Prewar Japan* (New Haven, 1966). While this surveys the growth of socialist political, labor, and agrarian organizations in Japan from as early as the 1890's, it concentrates on the period from 1925 to 1940 and pays particular attention to factional differences among the non-Communist parties of the left.

One exception to noting only English-language books may be permitted here, for it can be considered a constructive critique of the position of Ishida Takeshi in the selection translated and condensed for this volume. That is Matsuo Takayoshi, "Seitō Seiji no Hatten" (Development of Party Rule) in *Nihon Rekishi* (Japanese History), Iwanami Kōza, Gendai, II (Iwanami Symposium, Contemporary, II) (Tōkyō, 1963).

Only a few of the most relevant journal articles can be mentioned here. Sakata Yoshio and J. W. Hall, "The Motivation of Political Leadership in the Meiji Restoration," *Journal of Asian Studies* (*JAS*), XVI (November, 1956); Joyce C. Lebra, "Ōkuma Shigenobu and the 1881 Political Crisis," *JAS*, XVIII (August, 1959); Morris D. Morris, "The Problem of the Peasant Agriculturalist in Meiji Japan, 1873–1885," *Far Eastern Quarterly* (*FEQ*), XV (May, 1956): Ronald P. Dore, "The Meiji Landlord: Good or Bad?" *JAS*, XVIII (May, 1959); Douglas H. Mendel, Jr., "Ozaki Yukio: Political Conscience of Modern Japan," *FEQ*, XV (May 1956); and Bernard S. Silberman, "The Political Theory and Program of Yoshino Sakuzō," *Journal of Modern History*, XXXI (December, 1959).

For the whole question of what ideologies supplanted the liberalism of the 1920's in Japan, consult Ivan Morris, *Japan 1931–1945: Militarism, Fascism, Japanism?* in this series on "Problems in Asian Civilizations." That book was conceived as a companion to the present volume and also contains "Suggestions for Additional Reading."

With every passing year the output of scholarly articles, monographs, and other studies on modern Japan increases in a geometrical fashion. More Americans are becoming equipped with a control of the Japanese language so as to enable them to do their research directly in Japanese primary and secondary materials. They are influencing Japanese scholarship by their newly created methodologies, emphasis on empirical verification, and different biases. In American school and university curriculums Japan appears to be nip and tuck with China and India in the race of Asian civilizations for a place in our expanded American view of the world.

5 6 7 8 9 0